Please note that the video clips referred to in this book are now available online instead of on DVD.

Therefore, whenever you see a reference to DVD or , please refer to the videos at library.teachyourself.com.

To access the video clips, please follow the instructions below:

1 Visit library.teachyourself.com/redeem

2 Enter code **TYBSL01** and select 'Apply'

3 Check the code has been applied correctly. You will be prompted to sign in or create an account if you have not already done so.

4 Click 'Next'.

5 You can now access the video clips online, or download them to the Teach Yourself Library app.

Please note you will not be able to save the files to your computer.

T0385262

British Sign Language

Paul Redfern and Deafworks

First published in Great Britain in 2010 by Hodder & Stoughton. An Hachette UK company.

This edition published in 2016 by John Murray Learning

Copyright © 2010, 2016 Paul Redfern and Deafworks

The right of Paul Redfern and Deafworks to be identified as the Authors of the Work has been asserted by them in accordance with the Copyright, Designs and Patents Act 1988.

Database right Hodder & Stoughton (makers)

The *Teach Yourself* name is a registered trademark of Hachette UK.

British Library Cataloguing in Publication Data: a catalogue record for this title is available from the British Library.

ISBN: 9 780 34099 132 9

13

Cover image © Vladimir Mucibabic – Fotolia.com

Typeset by Cenveo® Publisher Services.

Printed and bound in Great Britain by CPI Group (UK) Ltd., Croydon, CR0 4YY.

John Murray Learning policy is to use papers that are natural, renewable and recyclable products and made from wood grown in sustainable forests. The logging and manufacturing processes are expected to conform to the environmental regulations of the country of origin.

Carmelite House
50 Victoria Embankment
London EC4Y 0DZ
www.hodder.co.uk

Dedication

To Deaf BSL tutors, who despite lack of materials, lack of professional development opportunities and lack of funding support still manage to maintain learning of BSL as one of the most popular evening classes in the UK.

Contents

Acknowledgements

Producing the book has been a complex exercise. We know the learner of a visual-spatial language will need to follow the text, the illustrations and the DVD clips to make good progress. The book's principal editor at Hodder, **Ginny Catmur**, has always understood the principles behind the book and has been enormously helpful throughout. Our grateful thanks go to her for her untiring support.

Completion of the learning pack has only been possible with a team of people:

Eleni Botonaki: The book relies heavily on our illustrator. As a Deaf BSL user herself, she was able to go straight into the technical aspects of how to draw the illustrations, and she has tirelessly worked to revise drawings in parallel with the revision of the text. Producing the book without a Deaf illustrator would not have been possible.

Ann Goldfinch: Ann has been working with BSL since 1981, teaching and assessing BSL to interpreter level; at present she is working as a freelance consultant, support tutor and assessor. She has helped us to finalize the text. Learners of BSL should have a learning resource of the highest quality, and producing this book would not have been possible without all the time she has given to the manuscript.

Suzannah Bartov: Suzannah took on the role of a learner and a proof-reader for the initial draft. Her role as an experienced (hearing) trainer enabled the text to be developed in a way which would be accessible to learners of BSL.

Antonia Maxwell, our editor, has worked through our manuscript with great care: and has enhanced our drafts with thoroughness and encouragement.

We regarded the DVD accompanying the book as essential from the outset: this has been efficiently produced by **AC2.com**. We have appreciated the enthusiasm with which **Joel Kellhofer** (Director of AC2) has approached the filiming and editing tasks involved. Three Deaf presenters are on the DVD – **Lee Robertson, Eleni Botonaki** and **Hannah Muriel** – and we appreciate all the hard work they put into bringing the book to life.

We have also benefited hugely from the advice and comments from many others, including: Don Stewart, Jeremy Condor, Fiona Harrup, Sandra Duguid, Claire Callow and Juliana Slobodian.

Credits

Front cover: © Vladimir Mucibabic – Fotolia.com

Back cover: © Jakub Semeniuk/iStockphoto.com,
© Royalty-Free/Corbis, © agencyby/iStockphoto.com, © Andy
Cook/iStockphoto.com, © Christopher Ewing/iStockphoto.com,
© zebicho – Fotolia.com, © Geoffrey Holman/iStockphoto.com,
© Photodisc/Getty Images, © James C. Pruitt/iStockphoto.com,
© Mohamed Saber – Fotolia.com

Meet the authors

Paul Redfern has worked with Laraine Callow and Nicholas Callow (Deafworks partners) on a wide range of projects over many years: in particular they have organized many highly regarded courses in BSL. Now recognized by linguists as a language, it is the most popular subject at evening class: but 35 years ago you would have had great difficulty learning British Sign Language (BSL); 45 years ago you would certainly have been told that BSL wasn't a language – just rather a crude system of gestures. The three authors have seen a huge change in attitudes towards the Deaf community's language over their working lifetimes.

The authors bring a range of different skills and experience to this book. Paul and Laraine, as Deaf professionals, have used BSL daily for all of their lives. Paul has decades of experience teaching it, and Nicholas, a course administrator, deals with hearing students of BSL. Paul and Laraine are trainers in a wide range of subjects related to deafness. As always they have drawn also on the skills and knowledge of others in the field to make this book on BSL as helpful to new learners of signing as possible, which they hope will be combined with much enjoyment.

Only got a minute?

A language that uses space, movement, direction to convey linguistic concepts. Different from spoken languages, and just as effective in transmitting ideas and emotions, doing this in a physical way that uses the hands, face and body in a dazzling blur of action.

That is BSL, the language of Deaf people living in the UK.

Unlike English, BSL is unique to the British Isles and is not international. It has an impressive historical pedigree, having been around for hundreds of years, ever since Deaf people started to congregate in groups to communicate with each other.

In BSL, the face replaces the voice, adding meaning to specific signs simultaneously, so one sign executed by the hands can change its meaning with a different facial expression. In this way, comments become questions and vice versa. This is similar to the way spoken language can change meaning with the use of a different tone.

Changing the orientation of a particular sign can also add meaning. An example would be the pronoun 'you': its singular form is the index finger pointing directly at one person; the same index finger sweeping in a horizontal arc indicates several people.

Similarly, speeding up the sign for rain would change it into the sign for heavy rain, and a change in the facial expression will also reflect this variation in the meaning.

Because many signs are used in conjunction with movement and facial expressions, and sometimes with orientation, ideas and thoughts can sometimes be transmitted faster than spoken languages.

None of this was known until the 1990s when, starting in the United States, research into the linguistics of sign language began, and as researchers delved deeper and deeper, it was found that all the above features had a common pattern (an essential for all languages) and could be recorded.

BSL – one of the four indigenous languages in the British Isles.

Only got five minutes?

The language of Britain's Deaf people – BSL.

Many people see BSL in action and are awestruck by the beauty of the juxtaposition of hands, body and face combining in smooth fluid motions to create thoughts or images.

Many people also want to learn, want to be able to share their thoughts using the same graceful movements. And the trend is growing – more and more people want to learn BSL. They want to be able to communicate with Deaf people, some for work-related reasons, some for enjoyment and social life, others because they have a Deaf relative and want to include them in the family.

Some, of course, take the learning to a high level and ultimately become sign language interpreters, working in a variety of settings. There is always a need for interpreters as Deaf people are involved in a wide variety of work in a range of posts.

Some people find it easy to learn, others less so. It requires the ability to see and observe the movements and to replicate these. Some people are natural signers, many others have to work to develop this skill.

BSL has a signing space, rules that govern the placement of signs, the varying speed of signs and facial expressions, a linguistic structure. One learner described it as similar to learning to drive a car in the early stages when one has to carry out a number of actions simultaneously.

BSL also varies in its dialects, just as spoken languages vary. There is ample scope for misunderstanding, which can be hilarious at times. It is also an evolving language, a language that grows in response to modern developments – for example, the sign for telephone has changed according to its shape and dimensions and use.

Young people also in common with hearing peers like to play with BSL, creating in essence a private language in front of adults, and there are specific groups that have their own jargon of signs.

It is inevitable, then, that the learner will struggle at times and wail: 'Why can't there be one sign for this word!' just as people learning English will rail against the vagaries of the English language. There is sometimes no discernible visual reason for a particular sign, or, maybe, the original reason has been lost over time. Some signs on the other hand are visibly clear and understandable, and give rise to the lie that BSL is simply a system of gestures – it is only when abstract concepts are used that this lie is exposed for what it is.

Compared to English, the rules of BSL are looser and more flexible. This is simply due to the flexibility of the space around the body, which the grammatical structure allows for expression and creativity. Again, the learner is likely to want to insist on strict rules – and will be disappointed.

Allied to any language is culture, and BSL is no exception. Conversations rely on unexpressed conventions that smooth the communication process. These need to be learnt and the learner's own conversational strategies need to be set aside. Culture is ever-changing, and Deaf culture also changes in response to the changing lifestyles of Deaf people, so what might be a fixed culturally accepted behaviour in one area will not necessarily be so in another.

Since it is a sign language based on visual and spatial concepts, it is not possible to find a sign for every English word; equally it is not possible to find an English word for every sign. The learner will need to learn those signs for which there is no clear translation by rote and by repeated practice.

Deaf people, like everyone else, vary in their ability to sign, and their BSL will also vary accordingly. Some will sign haltingly, with a heavy emphasis on English and mouthed words, others will sign sloppily and are difficult to understand, yet others will sign fluently and fast, with much less emphasis on mouthed words. When executed well and brilliantly, BSL can be raised to levels of startling beauty and expression.

At a deeper level, language is imbued with values, based on norms and conventions of the society it is used in. BSL signs also have values – again based on the norms of Deaf people that use it. Being a visual language, however, BSL signs tend to be descriptive with the face adding value. An example of this would be to describe someone as fat or thin, the signs themselves are descriptive but the face would convey whether this is a neutral comment, or whether it is made with approval or disapproval.

Fingerspelling is integral to BSL and often causes the most grief to learners. Learning to fingerspell is easy, reading is difficult. Reading fingerspelling calls for precision in understanding the various shapes and then combining these into an entity. It is similar to learning to read but on the hands. It is a skill that can be learnt separately from BSL and many young people do so when at school or in an out of school group.

Because BSL is based on visual-spatial concepts, it cannot be written into a form that is easily readable. For this reason, the best way to learn BSL is to either do it live or to watch DVDs. As with spoken languages, learning needs to be at the appropriate level – watching a recording of high-level BSL with the intention of learning will only succeed if the watcher is already at the same level.

In conclusion, BSL is a fast-changing language, sometimes beautiful, sometimes not. Sometimes it is mixed with English, but above all it is a language that challenges preconceptions and pre-set patterns of learning with its own flexible rules used by many people – not just Deaf people but also those who are friends, relatives or colleagues of Deaf people.

BSL allows for scope in creativity and space-enhancing descriptions in ways unavailable to spoken languages. It is exciting, fun and informative.

Welcome to BSL!

Foreword

British Sign Language (BSL) is a visual-spatial language, quite unlike the great majority of languages, which are spoken. Writing a *Teach Yourself* book about BSL has not been straightforward.

There are several books on the market about BSL. Many are based on a dictionary concept with pictures or photographs showing vocabulary lists of signs: they are worthwhile as a resource for those who have some understanding of BSL. There are also some books about the linguistic aspects of BSL written by academics and are extremely valuable as they get to the heart of what BSL is: the difficulty with these is that they tend to be too specialist for the ordinary learner.

We have been involved with the learning of BSL for decades, and have always felt the best way to learn is, as with all languages, to get to grips with the grammar of the language. Acquiring individual signs is relatively straightforward, but learners eventually become stuck because they haven't grasped how BSL is put together. This book combines both vocabulary and the linguistic aspects of BSL. It is an introduction to BSL for those who have never tried to learn BSL, although it should also enlighten those who are learning in a class or want to know a bit more about how the language works.

Paul Redfern

Laraine Callow and Nicholas Callow (Deafworks)

Introduction

About the course

Hello there! Want to learn sign language?

Welcome to an innovative book in the *Teach Yourself* series.

You may think there are plenty of signing books on the market, so why do we call this one innovative? It is because nearly all sign language books are either 'dictionary based', which show lists or groupings of individual signs (which are great for revision), or they are academic books focusing on the linguistic development of sign language (this is great too as the linguistic structure ('grammar') of sign language is still the topic of much research).

BSL stands for British Sign Language, which is the fourth indigenous language used in Britain. It is used by at least 70,000 people as their first language with several more thousands using BSL as their second or third language. Many are Deaf (see Chapter 1: 'Starting out with BSL structure' for explanation), but some are not.

For those of you wishing to learn BSL, *Teach Yourself BSL* is the right book for you. This is a self-study book that will enable you to understand and use some of the most essential elements of BSL.

This book does not follow a particular college course or one of the BSL curricula: but *Teach Yourself BSL* will complement any BSL training course you attend. In fact, your tutor may already have a copy of this book.

The key elements

There will be a strong focus on grammar. BSL is a visual-spatial language, and you will find it easier if you have someone to share the learning with; using sign language in conversation with another person will bring it to life for you.

Because BSL is a visual-spatial language, you will be expected to suspend your usual ways of communicating. For example, it is acceptable to point at things or people in BSL; it is not considered rude. Unlike learning spoken languages where you learn to listen, you will be learning how to observe and watch BSL.

There will be vocabulary as well as grammar. You'll be practising prepared dialogues so you can learn in blocks of language rather than a single sign at a time.

The structure of the book

Each chapter focuses on a specific area of BSL. The chapters should be taken in order if possible as each one builds on the previous one. Some concepts in later chapters will be difficult to learn if you have not already developed certain skills early on.

The book uses sign dialogues (conversations) and these have illustrations with descriptions. All dialogues are on a DVD so you can see how to sign correctly. You should work your way through each dialogue as these are designed to help you develop your skills. Without practising the dialogues you will not be able to develop your BSL. This is a new way of helping you, the student, to learn the basics of BSL. There are several weblinks you can use to look at some examples of signing, but at *Teach Yourself* we believe in giving you a helping hand in a very structured way.

Part of being a visual-spatial language is that the meanings of signs change in various ways. Precisely where signs are executed and how fast they are carried out are important features: therefore we strongly recommend you use the DVD with all dialogues.

There are also notes about Deaf culture, and these are designed to indicate how Deaf people's lives differ from those of the non-Deaf population.

Warning!

▶ *In the book the signs in BSL are drawn (usually this requires a series of drawings). Mostly we have also put the signs in English words: this is a beginners' book, and using English words like this we think will help you. BUT this is only to help you: you can't really write BSL in words, and putting it in words means a lot of BSL meaning is not expressed. In particular, you may think, seeing BSL in English words, that BSL is just a pidgin version of English: this is very far from the truth – as you hopefully already know BSL is a full and very rich language, but one which has a very different structure from English. Don't let the learning aid of having signs written as English words lead you into making false judgements about BSL.*

▶ *There will be inconsistencies at some points in the book (e.g. mouthing or not mouthing 'you') because, like all spoken languages, BSL has a very complex grammar (which includes borrowing structures from spoken English).*

Be successful at learning BSL

BSL is a visual and physical language. That means you are likely to be asking your body to do things that it is not accustomed to. For example, you may have some difficulty in moving your hands at the same time as blowing out your cheeks.

There are some similarities and differences to learning a foreign spoken language: for example, when you learn a foreign language you need to understand the culture of the country, the grammar, and the way that words are pronounced. With BSL you will be expected to learn about Deaf culture, use BSL grammar and understand how Deaf people use signs, using their faces and bodies to add meaning to the signs.

The main difference is that when you learn a foreign language, you use your ears to listen and your brain to comprehend unfamiliar sounds and to replicate those sounds when you speak. With BSL the process follows the same pattern but instead of using your ears you will use your eyes to understand what you see in order to replicate what you have observed.

Just as in learning any foreign language, you will learn faster if you can think in the new language, so try NOT to think in English as this will slow down your progress.

Some signs vary according to where you live: this can and does affect various signs you will see in this book and on the DVD. These individual signs may therefore not be an exact match of those used where you live. This should not be too much of a problem because as you work though this book you will acquire a good grasp of the principles of BSL and will therefore be able to adapt some signs accordingly. However, we do urge you to be flexible about learning more than one sign for a certain object or colour or number; follow what is in this book and do not be surprised if Deaf people local to you have a different sign: that is absolutely fine.

Here are some tips:

1 *Do practise doing the exercises even though they may feel strange or uncomfortable. The more you become comfortable with doing things, even though they may feel odd, the quicker you will pick up the essentials.*

2 *Avoid talking to yourself in English. BSL is not English and the more you stay thinking in English, the more difficult it will be to think visually. You will find yourself thinking in sounds and words, and that will slow your progress.*

3 *Look at people, watch their movements, including their mannerisms, and imitate them. The more you are able to copy people's movements, the quicker it will be for you to learn BSL as you watch Deaf people using signs.*

4 *BSL is a fluid language, which can express a great deal of subtlety of meaning. The illustrations are primarily a reminder (as in a dictionary): don't use them as a precise model. Signing involves movement so do use the DVD that comes with this book to see how signs move. If you are able to find a real life model – either a Deaf friend or a more experienced BSL learner – so much the better.*

5 *Don't aim too high when watching other DVDs or TV programmes. You will see sign language interpreters or Deaf presenters who are slick and highly proficient. Simply watch them for sheer enjoyment. Being realistic about what you can do is important and will help you to maintain your progress.*

6 *When you have worked your way through most of the book, do try to see if you can sign with a Deaf person. Many will welcome your efforts to communicate. And don't be afraid of making mistakes – you will learn from them.*

The final chapter of the book suggests where to go from here for further learning, and other possibilities.

Welcome to this ever-growing community of sign language users!

FEEDBACK

The authors will be glad to receive any comments about the book. As trainers we have always sought comments from course participants as we believe (and have found) these enable us to improve what we offer. Positive and negative comments always enable us to review what we offer in the future, and this applies as much to written work as to the workshops we have run.

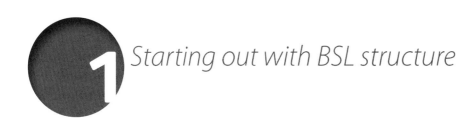

Starting out with BSL structure

In this chapter you will learn:
▶ *how to greet someone*
▶ *the importance of using your face in BSL*
▶ *about unmouthed words.*

We are going to introduce you to BSL and show you how it works.

Let's start straightaway with how we greet each other. If you can, find somebody who is interested to work with you. If this is not possible, you can still do this on your own. We will be using dialogues throughout this book (headed Dialogue).

DIALOGUE 1.1

First we will give the conversations in English, then show it in BSL. For example, here is the first dialogue in English:

> ✳ Hello, how are you?
> ● I'm fine, thanks.

Under each illustration we will write it in BSL (as far as we can because BSL is not a written language).

In BSL, we sign it like this *without using our voice*:

hello   ~~you~~   well?

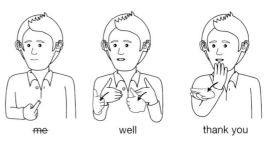

~~me~~   well   thank you

VOCABULARY

You will see this heading every time we introduce new signs.

 Clip 1

Now watch this clip. You don't need to copy the signing yourself yet if you don't want to: we are just introducing you to how signing works. There are five grammatical principles of BSL here:

1 You do not use your voice.

2 When you ask a question, you raise your eyebrows.

3 Some words are not spoken: this means you keep your mouth closed when signing.

For example, in the dialogue above:

▷ **You** (*you point at the other person and keep your lips closed*).

▷ **Me** (*you point at yourself and keep your lips closed*).

(raised eyebrows)

Try pointing to someone now without moving your mouth. This is not rude – it is a way of saying 'you' or indicating another person.

Deaf people feel that, because you are looking directly at the person you are signing to, there is no need to mouth 'you' or 'me', as your eye contact makes this obvious. That is why these words have been struck through (like this: 'me'), so you know that you should not mouth this but point or indicate a person.

4 The reply is 'me well thank you'. The other person will nod at the same time as signing this: this is called affirmation. The head nodding is carried out at the same time as the signing and not before or after. In BSL you use more than one action simultaneously. You will learn this throughout the book.

5 'Thank you' is carried out with one signing movement even though in English this is two words. You will find numerous examples of this throughout the book. Sometimes it will be two, three or four signs for one English word, and sometimes two, three or four English words for one sign. This is an important point to learn: *do not expect to substitute one sign for one word* – it just doesn't work because BSL and English are two different languages with different grammatical structures.

 Clip 1

Now go back to the DVD clip and copy the same dialogue again.

Throughout the book, in the illustrations attached to the dialogues, you will notice that for unspoken signs – like 'you' or 'me' – the face shows a neutral mouth position (you will not be speaking these words).

You will also notice that for mouthed signs – such as 'hello', 'well' and 'thank you' in the above dialogue – the illustrations will show an open mouth. This shows that the sign is mouthed (you say the word without using your voice).

(neutral mouth)

In this book, different ways of learning BSL are presented: you can look at the illustrations, follow the descriptions or check the DVD. But remember to practise again and again.

There will also be additional reminders of what you've learnt (headed Reminder).

(open mouth)

WORDS LEARNT IN THIS CHAPTER

hello
me
thank you
well
you

● INSIGHT: LEARNING TIP

Throughout the book, you can try quizzes, revisit aspects of your learning and do extra practice. These features can usually be found at the end of each chapter.

Things to remember

▶ You do not use your voice at all in BSL.
▶ Use your face for grammatical purposes.
▶ Some signs are unmouthed.
▶ Some combinations of English words can be incorporated into one sign.

2 More about Deaf people

In this chapter you will learn:
▸ *about Deaf culture and the language spectrum*
▸ *how to express affirmation and negation in BSL.*

2.1 D/deaf people

You will have noted that in the introduction, the capital 'D' was used for the word 'Deaf'. This is because most BSL users who are Deaf think of themselves as part of a cultural minority who use sign language as their first or preferred language. Deaf culture has many aspects – these will be pointed out as you work through this book. Look for these boxes:

> ● **INSIGHT: CULTURAL POINT**
>
> There are, of course, many people who have a hearing loss. The majority are people who lose sharpness of hearing as they get older. A few will have lost some or all of their hearing very suddenly. Most will have never used BSL. Many of them quite naturally will say, 'I'm very deaf' or 'I'm hard of hearing'. They will use the word 'deaf' with a lower case 'd'.

This book focuses on BSL (British Sign Language) – the language of those who consider themselves 'Deaf'. If you want to learn more about deafness and deaf people generally, enter 'deafness' or 'deaf awareness' into your internet search engine to locate further information.

People who are *not* d/Deaf are called 'hearing' people.

d/Deaf: some general differences

Deaf (capital 'D')	deaf (lower case 'd')
Deaf from birth or early age.	Usually lose hearing later in life.
First or preferred language is BSL.	First language is spoken (usually English).
See 'deafness' as normal.	See 'deafness' as disability or loss of hearing.
Enjoy meeting other Deaf people.	Want to maintain same circle of friends or family.
Pointing at people is not rude.	Often think pointing at people is rude.
Comfortable with being expressive.	Tend to be uncomfortable about using facial expressions.
Often check if other person is Deaf and uses sign language.	Tend to hide their own hearing loss.

Sometimes a Deaf person will ask somebody they have just met if they are Deaf or hearing. This is not seen as rude: it is so that the Deaf person knows whether to use BSL, write things down or to sign very slowly for a BSL learner.

DIALOGUE 2.1

Look at this dialogue in English:

* ✱ Hello, are you Deaf?
* ● No, I'm not Deaf, I'm hearing.

Now try this in BSL:

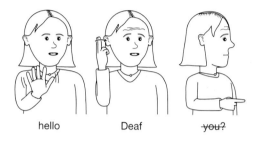

hello   Deaf   ~~you?~~

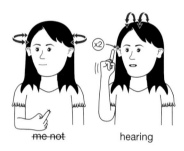

~~me not~~   hearing

When you say 'I am not deaf', make sure you shake your head at the same time. Practise this again. We use a ⊗ icon to indicate a repeated movement.

REMINDER

You will be using eye contact, therefore 'me' and 'you' are unspoken (the words '~~me~~' and '~~you~~' do not need to be said). Just remember to point.

 Clip 2

Now look at this clip on the DVD and practise the dialogue several times.

Some questions

Question	Answer
Why can't I use my voice?	In spoken English extra meaning is carried by voice (e.g. via intonation). The same extra meaning is conveyed differently in BSL: if you use your voice you will never learn BSL properly.
Why do I need to use my face?	You use your face in BSL in a grammatical way: just like you would use your voice in English to show various meanings.
I find it difficult to shake my head at the same time as I sign.	This is normal – just keep practising.
Can I substitute one sign for each English word I speak?	No: like any other language, the grammar and meanings differ in BSL.
Will it take a long time to learn?	It can do, but if you meet many Deaf people and practise a lot, you can learn the basics quickly.
I learnt the fingerspelling alphabet when I was young: will that help?	Yes: that will be covered in Chapters 11–15.

2.2 The language spectrum

Like everyone else, Deaf people vary. While many use BSL as their first or preferred language, there are some who do not use BSL but speak English with signs: this is usually called Signs Supporting English (SSE). Some people do not use signs at all, preferring to use hearing aids and speech.

To communicate with a wider range of Deaf people, it is best to learn BSL.

The language spectrum looks like this:

BSL   SSE (Signs Supporting English)   Spoken English

◄──►

● **INSIGHT: CULTURAL POINT**

Often a Deaf person meeting a new friend will check whether they sign. Again, this is not rude: it enables them to adapt communication quickly – see the dialogue below.

DIALOGUE 2.2

* Hello, do you sign?
* I sign a little bit.

Raise your eyebrows to show you are asking a question.

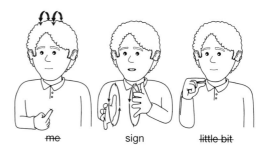

Nod your head at the same time to show you can sign.

 Clip 3

Watch this clip and practise the dialogue several times.

2.3 Affirmation and negation

▶ Affirmation is expressed by nodding the head.
▶ Negation is indicated by shaking the head from side to side.
▶ Using head nods/shakes appropriately will be more useful when meeting BSL users (Deaf people who use BSL).

EXERCISE

The use of head movements will be explored more as you progress but, for now, practise mouthing words and shaking your head using these words (we are not asking you to sign the words yet).

have

same

finish

before

Now do the exercise again, nodding your head instead.

QUIZ

1 What are people who are not d/Deaf called?

2 How do people who lose their hearing usually describe themselves?

3 Is pointing in BSL acceptable? Why?

ANSWERS

1 Hearing.

2 'Hard of hearing' or 'a little bit deaf'.

3 Yes: BSL is visual so pointing is part of the language.

WORDS LEARNT IN THIS CHAPTER

Deaf
hearing
little bit
sign

Things to remember

▶ Shake your head to add a negative meaning.

▶ Some words are unmouthed.

▶ Never use your voice.

▶ You can mouth two or three words but sometimes only need to use one sign.

▶ The same sign can be used as a question or as a statement, depending on the facial expression.

3 *BSL structures*

In this chapter you will learn:
▶ *word order in BSL*
▶ *mouth patterns in BSL.*

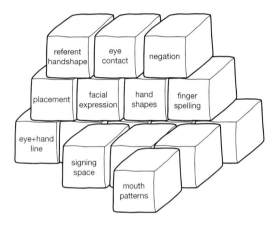

3.1 Word order

In Chapter 1 we said we would write the dialogues in English to help you understand the exchanges, but underneath the illustrations all text is written using BSL sign order. This not only helps you to learn the correct order when using BSL signs, but also enables you to think in BSL.

Translations

English	BSL
What's the time?	time what?
What's the weather like?	weather like what?
Why are you learning BSL?	~~you~~ learn BSL why?
What's your name?	~~you~~ name what?
Where do you live?	~~you~~ live where?
How did you get here?	~~you~~ arrive how?

Clips 2 and 3

Don't worry about the vocabulary just now; check the BSL sign order and watch the DVD clips again.

All these grammatical structures will be covered throughout this book in clear and simple stages so you gradually combine skills and develop fluency as you learn.

The word order in BSL is different from word order in English (just as every language has its own word order). BSL is considered a **simultaneous** language because it can show meaning using different strategies all at the same time (simultaneously). English, on the other hand, is a **sequential** language because one word follows another (in a sequence). The different, simultaneous nature of BSL is why it is so important to use its grammatical features correctly as well as its sign vocabulary. We will help you practise these all the way through the book.

BSL and English: some differences

BSL	English
Simultaneous	Sequential
Facial expressions	Voice tones
Signing space	No signing space
Expressions in signs	Expressions in voice

EXERCISE

Ask a friend to play charades with you. Don't use your voice: try to use facial expressions and gestures to enable your friend to guess what you are trying to convey. For example, you could try to act out the following:

▶ eating something you really dislike
▶ going out in the rain
▶ acting like Charlie Chaplin (or your favourite movie star).

Note: We are not saying BSL is like charades using gesture. The aim of this exercise is to make you aware of how you use other strategies when you are not using your voice. What strategies *did* you use with charades?

A further difference between English and BSL is that in English you often add extra words to add more meaning to a sentence: for example, to stress the difficulty: 'It was difficult' becomes 'It was very difficult'. In BSL, you don't add extra signs; instead you add facial expression (at the same time) and adjust the speed at which you sign (at the same time) in order to add extra meaning.

3.2 Understanding signs

BSL signs are often confused with gestures. You may be able to work out what some signs mean because they look like the actual object. Others cannot be worked out from how they are signed.

VOCABULARY

Here are two signs:

This is a simple movement showing a ball. It can be small or large. The size and shape of the ball are demonstrated by the hands. Copy this sign. How can you change the size of the ball?

ball

Now look at this sign which means 'sister':

'Sister' is a sign that is impossible to guess just by looking at it: it is created by a curved index finger tapping twice on the nose. Signs like this are impossible to know unless you have learnt them.

🔵 Clip 4

Look at the clip and copy the signs.

sister

Note: Many sign movements are made twice (like 'sister' above) so you will see an instruction '×2' which will tell you to repeat the sign movement.

It is essential to learn the vocabulary in this book as you go along as many signs will be hard to identify and must be learnt. The book will guide you through the intricacies of learning signing.

REMINDER

When you watch the DVD, note that there is no sound with the signing. You simply don't use your voice in BSL.

Question	Answer
Can you write BSL down completely?	No
Does BSL have a different structure from English?	Yes
Are all words translatable into signs?	No
Is BSL visual?	Yes
Must I use facial expressions?	Yes
Does the speed at which I sign change meaning?	Sometimes

3.3 Mouth patterns in BSL

A key skill of BSL is how the mouth is used. There are:

▶ unmouthed signs (the mouth remains closed)
▶ mouthed signs (the mouth articulates an English word but without voice).

UNMOUTHED SIGNS

Some signs are rarely mouthed. This is because their meaning is clear. Two examples with which you are already familiar are:

me
you

These are indicated by the words being struck through: e.g. '~~you~~'. To sign these, you simply point to the right person.

MOUTHED SIGNS: ENGLISH WORDS

Many signs will be mouthed without voice. For example, place names, which are always mouthed as though spoken in English, but no voice is used:

London

Doncaster

Brighton

EXERCISE

Try saying the above place names without your voice.

People's names and names of places, such as towns or countries, are always mouthed whether they are fingerspelt or signed.

There are other signs that are mouthed to avoid confusion as the same sign can be used for several different words e.g.

aunt

battery

nephew

niece

uncle

All these words use the same sign so the word needs to be clearly mouthed to show which word is being used. Copy the illustration and say each word (again, don't use your voice).

aunt/battery/nephew/niece/uncle

Similarly, the following signs are also mouthed:

always

sometimes

never

Don't worry about the signs just yet. Practise saying these words without your voice.

As you work through the book, you will learn which signs are mouthed or not mouthed: different mouth patterns will be highlighted, and it is recommended that you refer to the DVD so that you can see precisely how these are formed.

> ● **INSIGHT: LEARNING TIPS**
>
> Don't assume that all signs have one-word translations (one sign equals one word): they don't.
>
> Practise saying something (without the voice) with a head shake or a nod.
>
> Watch clips of signing on the internet or TV programmes: this will help you absorb how other Deaf people sign (we are not suggesting you will learn signing from these clips).

QUIZ

1 Which sign is easily identified – 'sister' or 'ball'?

2 Do some signs need to be mouthed because they represent more than one word?

3 Do you use your voice in BSL?

ANSWERS

1 'ball'

2 Yes. Examples are 'aunt', 'battery' and 'uncle': they are all signed in the same way – it is the mouth pattern that clarifies the meaning.

3 No

WORDS LEARNT IN THIS CHAPTER

aunt
ball
battery
nephew
niece
sister
uncle

Things to remember

▸ Think in BSL and not in English.

▸ BSL has a different word order to English.

▸ BSL is a simultaneous language.

▸ You can guess what some signs might be but not others.

▸ There is no need to say 'you' or 'me' when pointing.

▸ Some unrelated vocabulary shares the same sign.

4 Deaf culture and BSL etiquette

In this chapter you will learn:
▶ *about aspects of Deaf culture*
▶ *about the use of eye contact in BSL*
▶ *how to show you have understood*
▶ *how to start a conversation*
▶ *how to ask for clarification.*

4.1 Deaf culture

The word 'culture' is used here to mean 'way of life'. There are significant aspects of BSL that can be described as cultural and you will find pointers to these throughout the book. For example, we have already mentioned that Deaf people often ask a person if they can sign (see Chapter 2). In this chapter you will learn about BSL etiquette. These aspects will make your interactions with Deaf people more successful.

4.2 Eye contact

Deaf people use eye contact differently from hearing people. When you are watching another person sign, you must make sure you are looking at them; to look away breaks the flow of communication. You may have a cultural background that does not encourage eye contact during conversations. You may need to work at this to make sure you are watching the person signing. Looking away will indicate that you no longer wish to communicate (this is considered to be similar to putting your hands over your ears to stop hearing the person speaking to you) or watch the other person. Looking away whilst signing shows that the signer does not want to be interrupted.

Eye contact: some general differences

Deaf person	Hearing person
Watches the signing person intently.	Tends to look away when listening.
Looks away when arguing.	Eyeballs when arguing.
Looks at signing space when signing.	Tends to look at face when speaking.
Will stop signing if other person looks away.	Tends to keep on speaking, assuming other person is still listening.

4.3 Following a conversation

When you are watching someone signing, you must indicate that you understand them. This is called **affirmation** (showing that you understand). If you do not show understanding, the Deaf person will assume that you do not understand.

There are three main ways to show understanding:

▶ copying emotions/feelings (this is called **mirroring**)
▶ nodding/shaking your head
▶ using your hands to show understanding.

Copying emotions (mirroring)

This is simply reflecting another person's expressions. If they are showing happiness, you also smile; if they are showing sadness, you reflect their sad expression to show that you understand what they are saying.

Nodding/shaking head

This applies if someone is signing something. You can nod to show you understand, or if they sign something that wasn't very nice, you can shake your head to show that you agree it wasn't pleasant.

Using your hands to show understanding

This is either:

▶ a spread hand gently tapping on the chest and making a mouth similar to 'aha'

   or:

▶ an index finger gently wagging as if to say 'that's right', with a head nod.

aha!

 Clip 5

Watch the DVD to see how these affirmations are made.

4.4 Starting a conversation in BSL

In BSL, it is customary to raise your hand and wave it from the wrist with the palm facing downwards to attract the other person's attention so you can start a conversation.

If they are looking away and you want their attention, you tap them firmly on their shoulder using your finger-tips. Do not be too hesitant or heavy-handed.

The early chapters of this book will remind you to do this; later chapters will assume that you have successfully absorbed this into the opening of your conversations.

4.5 Checking in BSL

It is quite natural that, when you are learning BSL, you will not understand everything that is signed to you. You can ask 'again please'.

again   please

If you still do not understand, don't say 'again please' a second time. Look at following tips which will help you:

▶ Frown and tilt your head slightly to one side. The Deaf person signing to you will pick up that you haven't understood and will repeat what they signed.

▶ Be upfront and say: 'I'm sorry I don't understand'. Deaf people are generally more sympathetic to communication breakdowns because they experience it all the time. If they see you struggle, they will generally think of a way to make themselves understood.

(frown)

English: I'm sorry I don't understand.

sorry   ~~me~~   understand ~~no~~

REMINDER

The crossed-out words mean you do not mouth them but point and nod/shake your head: so don't mouth '*me*', just point to yourself. Also, the sign 'understand' is not a straightforward one: your finger and thumb are touching each other by the side of your forehead and then you 'flick' the fingers. Have a look at the DVD **Clip 6** and practise.

Ask a probing question, e.g. 'your friend – right?'. The signer will reply either 'yes' or 'no'. If 'yes', then you know you are on the right track. If not, then you can ask more questions to clarify.

The Deaf person signing to you will also know that you are having difficulty in following and may check with you from time to time.

 Clip 6

Watch the DVD clip again.

If you see a sign you don't recognize, you can ask 'what?'. The Deaf person signing to you will recognize that you haven't understood the sign and give you another that you may recognize, or they will fingerspell the word so you know what they are signing.

what?

QUIZ

1 How do you start a conversation in BSL?

2 When Deaf people argue, how do they use eye contact?

3 If you don't understand, what can you do with your face?

4 There are three ways to show you understand in BSL: what are these?

5 When Deaf people are 'listening' to you, do they look away or watch intently?

ANSWERS

1 By tapping on the shoulder or waving to attract attention.

2 They look away.

3 Frown – the person you are talking to will then repeat what they are saying.

4 By mirroring, using your head to nod or shake, or by using your hands.

5 Watch intently.

WORDS LEARNT IN THIS CHAPTER
again
aha!
please
sorry
understand
what?

Things to remember

▶ When you see Deaf people signing together, watch both the signer and the person watching the signer.

▶ Practise watching other people speaking without looking away.

▶ Frown and tilt your head when you don't understand.

▶ Learn how to tap people on the shoulder to gain their attention.

5 Introduction to facial expressions

In this chapter you will learn:

▶ *how to enhance meaning using facial expressions.*

5.1 Before you start

You will already know that the way you modify your voice is a very important part of your spoken language and communication. You change your voice to express anger, delight, disappointment or happiness; the whole range of emotions is expressed in your voice.

In BSL, the voice is not used: therefore any extra meaning or emotion is shown in a different way. You need to learn how to show the meaning of a sentence and how to demonstrate your feelings using your face. Your face is capable of changing meanings in a grammatical way and of showing a range of emotion. Your face is also capable of demonstrating what other people are feeling. Developing the ability to use facial expression to convey meaning, and to reflect someone else's emotion, is therefore a very important part of learning BSL. You can also copy other people's faces/emotions to show you understand what a BSL user is saying. This chapter and the ones immediately following will show you how you can develop accurate facial expressions which are also grammatical, and this will enhance your BSL.

5.2 Why learn facial expressions?

Hearing people sometimes use tone of voice to show their emotions or to ask questions. Deaf BSL signers use facial expressions to do the same. You need to move your face to express particular emotions and to change meanings of signs.

REMINDER

▶ Some facial expressions change the meaning of the sign.
▶ Facial expressions can add emphasis to the sign.
▶ They show emotions, either one's own or someone else's.
▶ Some head movements are affirmations ('yes') or negations ('no').
▶ You can show the other person whether you are following what they sign.
▶ English and BSL do not mix, so do not use your voice when signing.

5.3 Starting out with facial expressions

This section has three exercises. The aim is to enable you to feel in control of your facial movements, and to feel comfortable with moving your face more than you are used to.

EXERCISE

Find a mirror and look at your facial expression, keeping it blank to start with.

▶ Very slowly, without moving anything else on your face, raise your eyebrows as high as you can – and then relax.
▶ If you find that you are moving other features, try again and see if you can move your eyebrows on their own.

Once you have mastered raising your eyebrows, now move on to the next stage.

▶ Lower your eyebrows as low as you can.
▶ Then relax your face again.

Repeat this exercise until you have mastered it. Once you have achieved this, the next stage involves moving your mouth together with your eyebrows.

▶ Raise your eyebrows, hold and smile.
▶ Now slowly pull your mouth down while still keeping your eyebrows up.

You might have to practise this until you can keep your eyebrows up and pull your mouth down at the same time.

Do take time out to relax your face in between each exercise.

(eyebrows up, smiling mouth)   (eyebrows up, sad mouth)

▶ Now lower your eyebrows, and this time pull your mouth down.
▶ Lower your eyebrows again, and this time smile. Relax and then repeat.

Look at the illustrations if you get into a muddle.

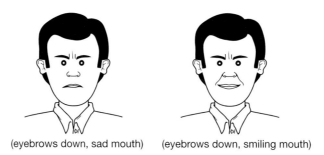

(eyebrows down, sad mouth)   (eyebrows down, smiling mouth)

Practise these exercises until you can do them all easily.

Using mouth patterns is an important feature in BSL. We will refer to different kinds of mouth patterns throughout the book.

EXERCISE: INTRODUCTION TO MOUTH PATTERNS

Here are some BSL mouth patterns for you to try with eyebrows up. Don't try to do all these exercises in one go! Have a break and come back to them later.

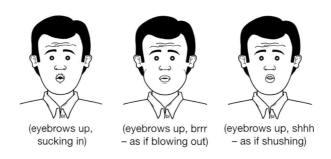

(eyebrows up,   (eyebrows up, brrr   (eyebrows up, shhh
sucking in)   – as if blowing out)   – as if shushing)

Here are three more mouth patterns:

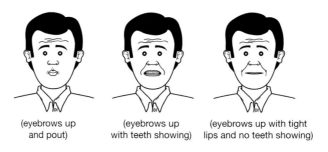

(eyebrows up   (eyebrows up   (eyebrows up with tight
and pout)   with teeth showing)   lips and no teeth showing)

Do the same exercises with your eyebrows down. The aim of these exercises is to help you to use your face confidently so you are in control of your BSL. These exercises will also help you to ask questions correctly in BSL.

EXERCISE

Here's another exercise in how to manage your facial expressions and stay in control. So far you have used six BSL mouth patterns, initially with eyebrows up and then with eyebrows down.

The next step is to add a further two movements: head shaking and head nodding. The aim is to combine three different elements at the same time – your eyebrows, your mouth and your head.

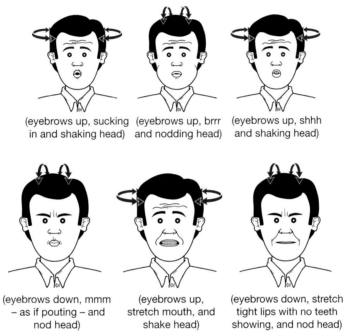

(eyebrows up, sucking in and shaking head)

(eyebrows up, brrr and nodding head)

(eyebrows up, shhh and shaking head)

(eyebrows down, mmm – as if pouting – and nod head)

(eyebrows up, stretch mouth, and shake head)

(eyebrows down, stretch tight lips with no teeth showing, and nod head)

Repeat these until you are comfortable using all three together. Vary the order if it helps. The essential point is to achieve control over the three elements of BSL: mouth patterns, eyebrows and head movements.

As with any form of muscular exercise that you may not be used to, relax your face in between tasks. By doing these exercises often and regularly at this stage you will enable your facial muscles to control your expressions better (and remember to include head shakes and head nods with these for practice).

You have now practised synchronizing your movements. Let's take this one step further, altering the speed of movement: using fast and slow movements:

▶ Using the same mouth patterns (ooo, brrr, shhh, mmm, etc.) and the same eyebrow expressions, which you hold still, shake your head (from side to side) very slowly.

▶ Now, gradually increase the speed until you reach a point where you cannot comfortably go any faster, then gradually slow down again – and relax.

▶ Repeat this exercise, only this time with your head nodding. When you have done this a few times, going from slow to fast and then back to slow, try moving your eyebrows up and down at the same time.

Things to remember

▶ Practise raising your eyebrows and dropping your mouth at the same time.

▶ Make sure that you are able to keep your eyebrows up, shake your head and make a pouting mouth at the same time.

▶ Practise varying your speed as you shake or nod your head while holding a mouth pattern.

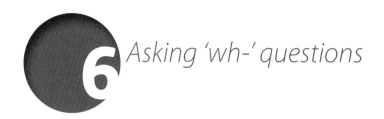

Asking 'wh-' questions

In this chapter you will learn:
▶ *how to ask 'wh-' questions.*

The everyday 'wh-' questions are usually asked with eyebrows down in BSL. As in English, the tone of the questions will vary according to the person you are talking to, where you are, what you are talking about and so on. For the moment, copy each sign and remember to keep your eyebrows down in a frown.

VOCABULARY

And the next three:

And finally:

 Clip 7

Now watch the DVD clip.

In spoken English **question words** nearly always begin sentences (e.g. '**How** are they?', '**Who** will be coming?'). For 'wh-' questions in BSL, these come at the end of the sentence.

So let's see how this works:

DIALOGUE 6.1

English:
* ✶ Good morning. Where do you live?
* ● I live in London. Where do you live?
* ✶ I live in Scotland.

good   morning

REMINDER

Your lips are an essential part of BSL: so when signing 'Good morning', you also silently mouth 'good morning' at the same time.

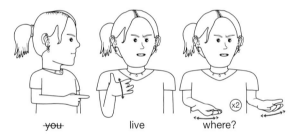

you   live   where?

me   live   London

you   live   where?

REMINDER

The question sign 'where' comes at the end of the sentence.

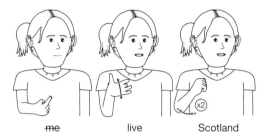

me   live   Scotland

Clip 8

Now watch the DVD clip and practise the dialogue several times.

DIALOGUE 6.2

Here's the next dialogue – first in English:

- ✳ Good afternoon. When is your holiday?
- ● I'm going on holiday tomorrow.
- ✳ Where are you going?
- ● France.

good   afternoon

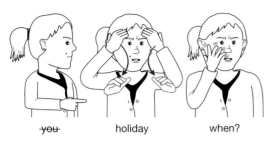

you   holiday   when?

me   holiday   tomorrow

holiday   where?

France

REMINDER

'me' and 'you' are not mouthed because 'me' and 'you' are reference points only, so you need to point at either yourself ('me') or to the other person ('you').

 Clip 9

Now watch the dialogue on the DVD clip.

> ● **INSIGHT: LEARNING TIPS**
>
> 'Wh-' question signs are usually at the end of a sentence.
>
> Many 'wh-' questions have eyebrows down.
>
> Sign and mouth 'good morning' at the same time with an expressive face.

QUIZ

1 Does the 'wh-' question sign come at the beginning or at the end of a sentence?

2 What does the illustrated sign for Scotland remind you of?

3 For 'wh-' questions do you have your eyebrows up or down?

ANSWERS

1 At the end of the sentence.

2 Bagpipes!

3 Eyebrows down.

WORDS LEARNT IN THIS CHAPTER
afternoon
France
good
good morning
holiday
how?
live
London
Scotland
tomorrow
when?
where?
which?
who?
why?

Things to remember

▶ Move your head at the same time as making mouth patterns, with eyebrows up or down.

▶ Use facial expressions with your signing.

▶ Use question signs like 'where?' and 'when?' at the end of the sentence.

▶ BSL is an expressive language using hands, face and mouth all at the same time.

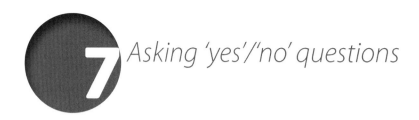

7 Asking 'yes'/'no' questions

In this chapter you will learn:

▶ *how to ask 'yes'/'no' questions.*

We have already covered 'wh-' questions, where you generally lower your eyebrows. Now let's look at other questions which, in BSL, generally use raised eyebrows. There are exceptions and variations depending on the mood, emotion and context: are you angry/sad? furious/puzzled? talking to your friend/colleague?

In English, we often ask a question expecting the answer 'yes' or 'no'. In BSL, you raise your eyebrows when you ask questions expecting 'yes' or 'no'. The other person replies using the same sign but with neutral eyebrows: nodding gives the answer 'yes' and shaking the head gives the answer 'no'.

Let's practise what we mean by looking at four short dialogues.

(raised eyebrows)

REMINDER

We give the dialogue in English and then give you the BSL version to the right as well as under each illustration. This will help you think in BSL.

DIALOGUE 7.1

English:	BSL:
✶ Are you Deaf?	✶ Deaf ~~you~~?
● Yes, I'm Deaf.	● Deaf ~~me~~

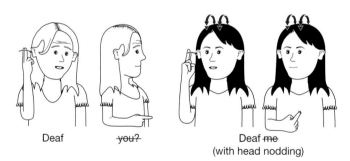

Deaf ~~you?~~   Deaf ~~me~~
(with head nodding)

DIALOGUE 7.2

English:
* ✱ Are you hearing?
* ● No, I'm not hearing.

BSL:
* ✱ hearing ~~you~~?
* ● hearing ~~no~~

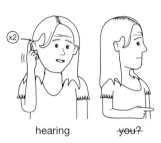

hearing   ~~you?~~

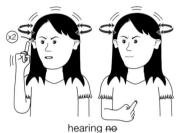

hearing ~~no~~
(with head shaking)

DIALOGUE 7.3

English:
* ✱ Are you married?
* ● Yes, I'm married.

BSL:
* ✱ married ~~you~~?
* ● married ~~me~~

married   ~~you?~~

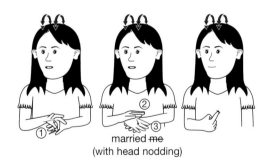

married ~~me~~
(with head nodding)

REMINDER

Nodding your head means affirmation.

DIALOGUE 7.4

English:
* ✳ Do you like sport?
* ● No, I don't like sport

BSL:
* ✳ like sport ~~you~~?
* ● ~~don't like~~ sport

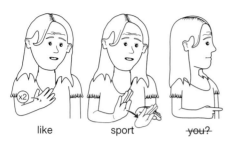

like   sport   ~~you?~~

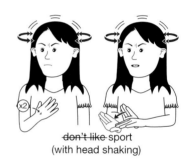

~~don't like~~ sport
(with head shaking)

REMINDER

Point instead of saying 'you' or 'me' and shake your head to make a negative, e.g. 'I don't like …'.

 Clip 10

Now watch the DVD clip and practise several times.

DIALOGUE 7.5

Let's use this in another dialogue.

English:
* ✳ Hi! Are you Deaf?
* ● No, I'm hearing. I'm married to a Deaf person.
* ✳ Oh, I see! Nice to meet you.
* ● Nice to meet you too.

BSL:
* ✳ hi Deaf ~~you~~?
* ● ~~no me~~ hearing married Deaf (person)
* ✳ aha! nice meet you
* ● same, nice meet you

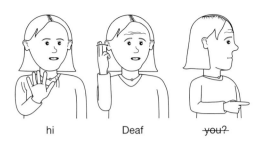

hi   Deaf   ~~you?~~

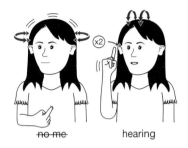

~~no me~~   hearing

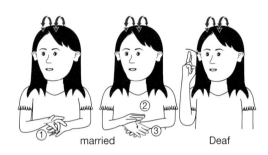

married   Deaf

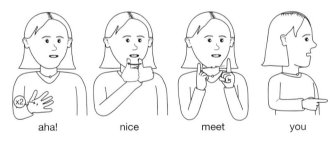

aha!   nice   meet   you

same   nice   meet   you

REMINDER

Do not use your voice!

 Clip 11

Now watch this dialogue on the DVD clip.

WORDS LEARNT IN THIS CHAPTER
like
married
meet
nice
sport

Things to remember

▶ You can use the same grammatical structure for either questions or statements.

▶ To sign a statement responding to a question you indicate with either a nod or a shake of the head.

▶ You can change the meaning of a sign or phrase by raising your eyebrows or by nodding your head.

▶ It is customary for Deaf people to be direct in their personal questions.

▶ You need to be able to use your mouth, face and head simultaneously, without using your voice.

8 More about questions

In this chapter you will learn:

▶ *how to ask leading questions*
▶ *how to turn questions into answers*
▶ *some BSL grammar points.*

8.1 Asking leading questions

Some questions are in fact leading questions: the questioner expects a specific reply of 'yes' or 'no'. For example, 'You have got a hat, haven't you?' implies that you know the person does have a hat and you want more information. In BSL, leading questions also require raised eyebrows.

Look at these questions:

English translation	BSL
Have you got a bike?	bike have?
Will you go shopping?	go shopping will?
Have you been to America?	America been?
Can I watch sport?	watch sport can?

REMINDER

The question signs 'have', 'will', 'can' and 'been' are used at the end of the question.

bike   have?

go   shopping   will?

America   been?

watch   sport   can?

Clip 12

Now watch the DVD clip. Some of the signs are hard to do, such as 'been' and 'can', so study them carefully and practise until you feel comfortable.

8.2 Turning questions into answers

You can respond to questions by using the same signs but change the meaning by using a different facial expression or head movement.

DIALOGUE 8.1

English:
* ✳ Have you been shopping?
* ● Yes, I've been shopping.
* ✳ I bought some clothes and food.
* ● Oh, I see!

BSL:
* ✳ shopping been?
* ● shopping been
* ✳ buy clothes food
* ● aha!

shopping   been?

shopping   been

Nod to show affirmation.

buy   clothes   food

aha!

🔘 Clip 13

Now watch this on the DVD clip.

8.3 BSL grammatical structure

Deaf people tend to use the sign 'been' as a way of showing that something has already happened.

Look at how these BSL sentences translate into English:

BSL	Translation
shopping, been?	Have you been shopping?
shopping (*with head nodding*) been	Yes, I've been shopping.
buy food been	I bought some food.

However, a key concept to remember is that BSL is not English, and vice versa: while there is some cross-over, they are still two separate languages. So don't use your voice: it anchors you in the 'English' mode of thinking.

EXERCISE

You have already learnt the signs below: check with the illustrations and the DVD to make sure you know them.

▶ Sign the question with eyebrows raised.
▶ Repeat the question to answer 'yes' (head nod as you sign).
▶ Repeat the question to answer 'no' (head shake as you sign).

Question	Answer
food have?	have food
bike have?	have bike
shopping been?	been shopping
Scotland been?	been Scotland
London been?	been London
Deaf you?	Deaf me
hearing you?	hearing me
married you?	married me
same?	same

If you are practising this with a friend, take it in turns to ask the questions and reply both negatively and positively.

WORDS LEARNT IN THIS CHAPTER

America	go
been	have
bike	shopping
buy	TV
can	watch
clothes	will
food	

Things to remember

▶ BSL and English are two separate languages.

▶ Leading questions have eyebrows raised.

▶ Question signs are usually used at the end of a sentence.

▶ Occasionally, English words are integrated into BSL.

9 How to use facial expressions

In this chapter you will learn:

▶ *how to change meaning using facial expressions*
▶ *how to use your face to express affirmation/negation.*

9.1 Using your face to change meanings

Having practised the facial exercises, you should now be comfortable using your face to ask questions or make simple statements. In this chapter you will learn how to change your facial expression so that, when using the same sign, you can mean different things. One example is the sign 'same', which you can mouth without using your voice.

English: 'It's the same.'

same

English: 'Is it the same?' (remember to use 'eyebrows up' to make it a question).

same?

You can also add more emphasis by tilting your head slightly.

You can agree by nodding your head: 'Yes, it's the same.'

same
(head nod)

You can disagree by shaking your head: 'No, it's not the same.'

same
(head shake)

Clip 14

Now watch the different ways of using this sign.

These different ways of signing 'same' illustrate the flexible nature of BSL, and how facial expressions can change the meaning of the sign. The same principle can be used with a range of signs. The more confident you are in being able to use facial expressions in this way, the easier it will be for you to acquire the basics of BSL.

DIALOGUE 9.1

Let's see how this works in a dialogue.

Two people are food shopping; they are comparing the price of a carton of fruit juice:

English:	BSL:
✳ Are these both the same?	✳ same?
● No, they're not the same. They are a different price.	● same ~~no~~ (*head shake*) price different
✳ But don't they look the same?	✳ look same
● They do look the same!	● look same (*nod*)

same?

same ~~no~~   price   different

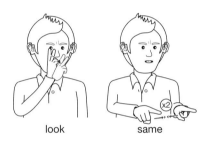

look   same

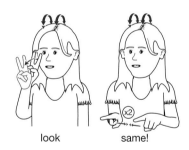

look   same!

💿 **Clip 15**

Now watch this on the DVD clip.

9.2 Using your face for affirmation or negation

Earlier you learnt that in BSL you can show affirmation/negation through the use of facial expressions or some signs.

DIALOGUE 9.2

This dialogue shows *how* you can demonstrate you do not fully understand the other person by frowning: take particular care in studying the dark-haired person in the illustration. Notice she does not sign 'I don't understand', she frowns and tilts her head slightly to show she does not understand the question. Try this yourself by practising several times.

English:	BSL:
✳ Where's the shop?	✳ shop where?
● Sorry I don't understand.	● *(frown and tilt head)*
✳ Where's the food shop? I want to buy some food.	✳ food shop where? want buy food
● Oh right, it's straight on.	● ~~oh right~~ *(closed hand movement)* straight on
✳ Thank you.	✳ thank you

shop ⟷→where?←⟷

(frown)

food   shop   ⟷→where?←⟷

want   buy   food

oh right   straight on

thank you

🎞 Clip 16

Now watch this dialogue.

● INSIGHT: LEARNING TIPS

When watching the clip (or a situation where there are Deaf people signing to each other), watch both people. In particular watch the person who is *looking at the signer,* to see how they both affirm or negate using facial expressions.

Practise different expressions using one sign, e.g. try signing 'different' with head nod or head shake.

Frown and tilt your head when you don't understand and need the other person to repeat.

WORDS LEARNT IN THIS CHAPTER

buy	price
different	shop
food	straight on
look	thank you
oh, right	want

Things to remember

▶ You can vary signs with a range of facial expressions.

▶ In BSL, there is no need to mouth 'yes': this is shown by nodding.

▶ You usually mouth the words 'same', 'look', 'price' and 'different'.

▶ You can show you don't understand the speaker by frowning.

▶ Use head nods or shakes in response to questions.

10 BSL mouth patterns

In this chapter you will learn:
▶ *how to use mouth patterns for emphasis.*

10.1 Introduction to mouth patterns

BSL mouth patterns add extra information to actions, descriptions or emphasis. They can feel strange to do but you will get used to them. Here are some common examples:

▶ The English sentence 'The weather is hot' would be signed 'weather hot' with the mouth pattern 'ooo'. This mouth pattern adds extra information to the 'hot' sign. Look at the illustration and copy the expression.
▶ If you want to show that the weather is *very* hot then you need to blow out your cheeks: the puffed cheeks show extra emphasis.

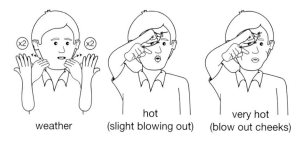

weather

hot
(slight blowing out)

very hot
(blow out cheeks)

▶ In contrast, for 'The weather is cold', the 'cold' sign would be signed with a mouth pattern similar to a soundless 'brrr'. Again cheeks puffing outwards will show the extra emphasis, changing the meaning from 'cold' to 'very cold'.
▶ 'The weather is freezing' would be signed 'cold' with a mouth pattern similar to 'brrr' but blowing out more emphatically, and the signing would be made faster to show the increased emphasis from 'cold' to 'freezing'.

cold (short prrr)   very cold (longer prrr)   freezing (intense prrr)

► A different mouth pattern is 'shhhh', which is a combined sign and mouth pattern meaning 'not yet'. It is linked to time, in particular something that has not yet happened. See the dialogue below where it is used to answer a question. Study the illustration in Dialogue 10.1 and copy the sign.

Clip 17

Check both the illustrations and the DVD clip so you can see precisely how all these mouth patterns are formed.

Let's practise with a new dialogue:

DIALOGUE 10.1

English:	BSL:
✳ Have you been to France?	✳ France been?
● Not yet.	● ('shhhh' mouth pattern)
✳ Why?	✳ why? (frown)
● The weather is really cold.	● weather ('oooh' mouth pattern) freezing
✳ Oh, I see!	✳ aha!

France   been?

shhh

why?

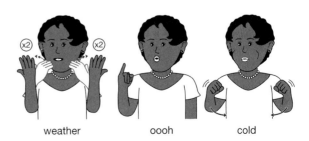

weather   oooh   cold

aha!

 **Clip 17**

Now watch this on the DVD clip.

REMINDER

None of these mouth patterns is linked to English mouth patterns. They are important so do practise them several times. The key point is that ALL these mouthed signs do not use voice.

10.2 Grammar revision

▶ The BSL mouth pattern 'brrr' can be used to strengthen the sign 'cold' so that it means 'very cold'. Similarly, the mouth pattern 'ooo' can be used with the sign 'hot'.

▶ The BSL mouth pattern 'shhh' is used with the sign for 'not yet' to show that something hasn't happened yet.

▶ The facial expression using the puffing out of cheeks is used for extra emphasis when signing 'weather is very hot' (or 'very cold').

WORDS LEARNT IN THIS CHAPTER
been
cold
France
freezing
hot
not yet
weather
why?

Things to remember

▶ The BSL mouth patterns 'ooo' and unvoiced 'brrr' are used for emphasis, for example for 'very hot' and 'very cold'.

▶ The BSL mouth pattern 'shhh' is used with a sign to show that something has not happened yet.

▶ 'Aha' is used to show understanding.

▶ Use your face to express different emotions and as a means of affirmation or negation.

▶ Exercise control over facial expressions and head movements.

▶ Use facial expression and head tilt when you don't understand.

11 *Starting out with fingerspelling*

In this chapter you will learn:

▶ *the basic rules of fingerspelling.*

11.1 Before you start

In fingerspelling we use hands and fingers to create the letters of the alphabet: you literally spell words using your fingers. In this and the next chapter you will learn how to fingerspell. Later, you will also learn important techniques for *reading* fingerspelling so that you will be able to communicate easily with BSL users.

You may have come across fingerspelling when you were younger at a children's club. As you go through the following exercises you will gain fluency and be able to fingerspell with a pleasant rhythm.

In English, each letter on its own carries little meaning; only when other letters are added does it begin to make sense. For example, the following letters do not have any meaning:

> **T t a a t o h n h a e c t m t e s**

The letters are all there but they have been scrambled.

But can you recognize this sentence?

> **Th ct at on he ma**

You do not need to see every letter to grasp that this is the phrase, 'The cat sat on the mat'. So in fingerspelling:

▶ You do *not* need to see every letter to understand the whole name or word that you are reading.

▶ You do not need to fingerspell everything perfectly for the other person to grasp the meaning.

▶ Although accuracy is always desirable, it does not matter if the name is fingerspelt Peetr (Peter) or Ptera (Petra), as long as you recognize what you are seeing.

In the following chapters you will alternate between learning to fingerspell and learning to *read* fingerspelling.

11.2 Why learn to fingerspell?

Some people learn fingerspelling without learning BSL. However, fingerspelling is included in this book for the following reasons:

▶ Some BSL signs are dependent on fingerspelling.
▶ Some places and names do not have signs and need to be fingerspelt.
▶ Some Deaf people (especially older people) use fingerspelling more than signs (though this is becoming less common).

Fingerspelling is therefore an important part of BSL even though it can be learnt separately.

11.3 Fingerspelling: basic rules

BSL fingerspelling is two-handed, using an active hand and a passive hand. So if you are right-handed, then your left hand is passive. This book will mainly show illustrations of a right-handed person fingerspelling (for more on this see Chapter 12).

When fingerspelling you always mouth the name or word as you spell it.

Do NOT say the individual letters. For example, when you fingerspell C A T, you say 'cat' and not 'see ay tee'.

Don't use your voice.

HAND POSITION
▶ Hold your hands as if you were carrying a small bowl in front of you, with your elbows slightly tucked in (but not too tight).
▶ Open out your left hand (this is your **passive** hand).
▶ Close your right hand (your **active** hand) so that only the index finger sticks out.

open hand   closed hand with index finger

LEFT-HANDED PEOPLE

If you want to fingerspell left-handed, then use your right hand as your passive hand and the left hand as your active hand.

Once you have decided which hand you prefer as your active hand, stick to it. It will make learning easier.

Things to remember

▶ Fingerspelling involves whole names or words.
▶ There are two types of handshapes – an open hand and a closed hand.
▶ Fluency is better than speed.
▶ There are some signs in BSL that are fingerspelt (called 'fingerspelt signs').

12 Learning to fingerspell

In this chapter you will learn:

▶ *the fingerspelling alphabet.*

This chapter is broken up into sections to encourage you to work through the chapter slowly and practise your fingerspelling thoroughly as you go along.

In the previous chapter you learnt about the correct hand positions for fingerspelling.

● ARE YOU LEFT HANDED?

Most of our illustrations will show right-handed fingerspelling, so if you are left-handed you will need to interpret these to match your fingerspelling correctly. We give you a couple of examples in the first two illustrations to start you off.

Let's start with some numbers (note: numbers are not normally fingerspelt – we are using numbers here just for practice). This is the right-handed version of 'one':

If you are left handed then 'one' looks like this:

The right-handed fingerspelling for 'two' is:

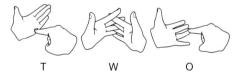

If you are left handed then 'two' looks like this:

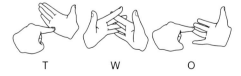

Clip 18

Now check your fingerspelling on the DVD clip.

Now that you know five letters, here are some words to practise:

won	**ton**
none	**tone**
tow	**new**
net	**ten**

The aim is that you should feel comfortable. Speed is not important; fluency is, so practise these words until you feel you are getting the hang of them. Then try with your eyes closed!

REMINDER

Mouth the words (e.g. 'net', 'ten', etc.) as you fingerspell them – not letter by letter.

This is a very important stage because you need to develop accuracy and to be relaxed and comfortable with fingerspelling before moving on. So, if you are still struggling to work out where to put your index finger, go back and keep practising until you have mastered it. If you are feeling relaxed and are able to place your index finger correctly, then it's time to move on.

TWO MORE NUMBERS

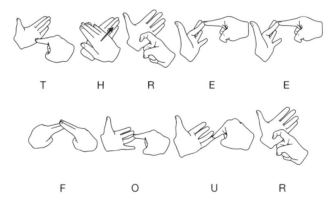

T   H   R   E   E

F   O   U   R

 Clip 19

Compare your fingerspelt words with the DVD clip.

Here are some more words for you to practise fingerspelling:

when	**town**
tour	**throw**
few	**feet**
frown	**reef**

Again, practise these until you can do them without looking at your passive hand and without wondering where to place the index finger of your active hand. Don't forget to mouth each word (not letter) as you fingerspell it – and remember not to use your voice.

You may begin to feel that your left hand is a bit too stiff. That's fine: you can move your left finger a little to meet your right index finger (just a little movement though). Practise this.

(showing slight movement of 'e')

Clip 20

Check your finger movements with the DVD clip.

EXERCISE

▶ Move your right index finger to touch the thumb and then to the little finger of your left hand.

▶ Repeat this until it feels natural. Your left-hand thumb and little finger will move slightly to meet your right index finger.

▶ Now try it the other way round, starting on the little finger and moving to the thumb. This is not so easy, but keep that finger and thumb moving to meet the index finger.

If your passive hand is flexible, it will make it easier to achieve fluency.

****

Let's continue with more numbers (remember we are using numbers for practice only: you do not usually fingerspell numbers).

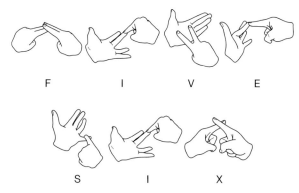

F   I   V   E

S   I   X

Now there are even more words you can fingerspell. Remember to mouth the whole words and not to say individual letters.

hex	**fit**
vine	**stiff**
wives	**fix**
rites	**vixen**
event	**tennis**

Clip 21

Check your fingerspelling with the DVD clip.

Keep practising until you are able to spell smoothly and without having to look at your fingers. There should be no pause between any of the letters, otherwise the last four words would look like this:

rit   es   **eve   nt**
vix   en   **ten   nis**

CLARITY NOT SPEED!

At this stage it doesn't matter if you are slow – as long as you keep a steady consistent pace and that your fingerspelling is smooth and not erratic or broken up. Keep practising until you can fingerspell accurately with your eyes shut.

WANT TO TAKE A BREAK?

At this stage you may want to go on to the next chapter ('Reading fingerspelling'), especially if you are practising this with a friend. When you have read it, return to this section and finish this chapter.

****

Here are some more numbers (we won't cover 'seven', 'nine' and 'ten' as we have already practised these letters).

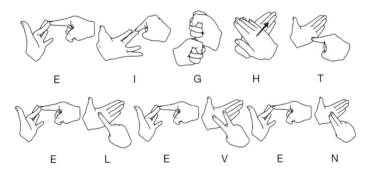

You can combine these letters to make more words – remember to mouth them as full words as you go along:

line   **still**
lives   **file**
light   **gel**
height   **fight**

Clip 22

Look at the DVD clip.

Now that you have 15 letters (more than half the alphabet), let's clear up any potential confusion:

▶ The 'T' and 'L' sometimes look like each other, but the 'T' prods the side of passive hand with the fingertip, while the 'L' has the whole finger resting on the palm.

▶ The 'N' and 'V' both have two fingers resting on the passive hand, but with the 'N', the fingers are kept together.

Clip 23

Doublecheck these points on the DVD clip.

> ● ALERT!
>
> Are you able to fingerspell smoothly without hesitation and with your eyes closed? If not, keep practising. You will need this skill for the next section.

****

So far 15 letters have been covered; now learn another 6 letters and that will leave 5 more to complete the alphabet.

Try these two words (which are not numbers):

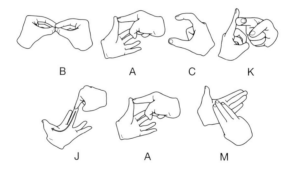

B   A   C   K

J   A   M

Clip 24

Use the DVD clip for reference.

****

This time instead of fingerspelling words, let's spell out some names, which is what Deaf people mainly use fingerspelling for. You have practised most of the letters now.

Sam	**Sascha**
Matt	**Rhiannon**
Klaas	**Shakira**
Javier	**Geena**
Francesco	**Jeannette**
Steve	**Maeve**
Jack	**Christina**

REMINDER

Keep your left hand flexible, i.e. move your left-hand fingertips slightly to meet your right-hand index finger (vice versa for left-handed people).

****

Now you can finish learning the alphabet.

Here are the last five letters, using a name and a word:

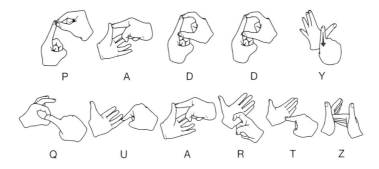

Practise the last few letters by fingerspelling the following place names in the UK:

Pinxton	**Queensbury**
Aylesbury	**Azerley**
Deal	**Denby**

REMINDER

BSL users generally use fingerspelling for places and names.

Here are some more names to practise your fingerspelling with:

Zac	**Marlee**
Bradley	**Whoopi**
Aaliyah	**Didier**
Anaya	**Ronaldo**
Beyonce	**Dimitar**
Odalys	

Clip 25

Again, this DVD clip is here to help you.

****

Fingerspelling is also used to sign other words, e.g. days of the week. These are called 'fingerspelling signs'. We will look at these in more detail in Chapter 14.

QUIZ

1 When you tap the middle finger – what vowel is this?

2 What do you do with your mouth when fingerspelling?

3 For left-handed people, which hand is the passive hand?

4 Why is it better to learn in words or names than letter by letter?

ANSWERS

1 'I'

2 Mouth the word or the name at the same time.

3 The right hand.

4 Because this is how we think and it helps us to learn faster.

Things to remember

▶ In fingerspelling there is an active and a passive hand.

▶ Fluency is more important than speed.

▶ You can move the fingers and thumb of your passive hand slightly to meet the index finger of your active hand.

▶ You spell in words, not letter by letter.

▶ You mouth each word as it is spelt, without voice.

▶ It's important to be able to fingerspell without looking at your hands or hesitating where to place your index finger.

▶ Fluency is better than speed – keep a steady pace.

13 Reading fingerspelling

In this chapter you will learn:

▶ *how to read fingerspelling.*

13.1 Learning to observe correctly

A common mistake when reading fingerspelling is to look only at the hands. As you learnt in Chapter 5 ('Introduction to facial expressions') there is a lot of information portrayed on the face. Your focus should therefore be primarily on the other person's face while still being able to see their hands.

You are more likely to understand what is being fingerspelt if you also look at the lips. If you need clarification, you then look carefully at the hands in order to get the word or name right.

Stand back so that you can see the other person from head to waist. You should be able to see their face as well as their hands and upper body. There is a lot of information happening in these areas.

If you find yourself only looking at the hands, you are probably too close: step back so you can see the face and the hands at the same time.

If you are looking at the mouth and hands at the same time, and the other person is mouthing 'Vee Own Aah' with the letter 'F' on the hands, you will grasp it is the name Fiona. In the same way, if the other person is mouthing 'Ah Meh D' and you see the letter 'A', it will be Ahmed, so make sure you can see both the hands and the mouth.

REMINDER

Look at both the mouth and the fingerspelling.

Now for some suggestions to help you read fingerspelling. Here are three different tactics to help you:

13.2 Tactic 1: think phonetically

When people learn to fingerspell, there is a tendency to think letter by letter. This book has structured your learning in such a way that you learn in words as explained in Chapter 11 ('Introduction to fingerspelling'). A good technique for reading fingerspelling is to read the word phonetically (e.g. by sound), using your own memory to recreate the sounds of the groups of letters. That means you don't read it letter by letter, you read it as a complete word.

For example, if the letters are M and A, don't say them as separate letters like 'M', 'A', say them as 'Ma'.

EXERCISE

Thinking phonetically, see if you can complete the names of these places in the UK:

L	O	C	A
N	O	H	A
G	L	B	O
P	E	L	I

What did you get? Most likely you thought of some of the following names:

Loughborough, Lowestoft, London
Norwich, Nottingham, Northampton
Glasgow, Glastonbury, Gloucester
Perth, Penrith, Peterborough
Cardiff, Carlisle, Cambridge
Harrogate, Hastings, Halifax
Bournemouth, Bolton, Boston
Liverpool, Lincoln, Lichfield

You might have worked out most of the names even though you only have the beginning of each name. Using your knowledge in this way enables you to get on track using the sound of the first few letters only.

13.3 Tactic 2: first/last technique

Let's look at another tactic. This is called 'first/last technique'.

Here is a well-known and often quoted paragraph as an example of how our brains are able to make sense of jumbled words. See if you can read it.

Aoccdrnig to a rscheearch at Cmabrigde Uinervtisy, it deosn't mttaer in waht oredr the ltteers in a wrod are, the olny iprmoetnt tihng is taht the frist and lsat ltteer be at the rghit pclae. The rset can be a total mses and you can sitll raed it wouthit porbelm. Tihs is bcuseae the huamn mnid deos not raed ervey lteter by istlef, but the wrod as a wlohe.

Notice that the first and last letters of the words are correct, so if you can read this you are using the 'first/last technique'. If you can train your brain to use this technique when reading fingerspelling, you will be able to read it well.

Here are some blank names. Look at the first and last letters and see how many names you can come up with.

R   D
A   A
M   N
S   H

You don't know if these are names of people or places, so let's narrow it down a bit. They are all people and:

R   D (is a male name)
A   A (is a female name)
M   N (is a male name)
S   H (is a female name)

Here are some options:

Richard, Rashid, Ronald, Raymond
Amanda, Amelia, Anna, Alexandra
Martin, Mervyn, Marlon, Marvin
Sarah, Susannah, Shelagh

There are two important things to learn from this:

▶ It is a lot easier to work out what is being fingerspelt if you know whether the name is female or male.
▶ Once you know the first and last letters of the name, you will have some possibilities to work out by using the 'first/last technique'.

● **INSIGHT: CULTURAL POINT**

If you use fingerspelling, many Deaf people will appreciate that you are taking the trouble to learn it. With the skill of fingerspelling in addition to signing, you will be able to have a short conversation.

13.4 Tactic 3: ask for clarification

You have learnt two tactics to help you read fingerspelling. You have also learnt that fingerspelling is easier to follow if you know the context.

In Chapter 4 ('Deaf culture and BSL etiquette'), it was stressed that asking 'again please' is unhelpful as this does not:

▶ give you more information about the fingerspelt word/name (for example, is it a place, a person or an object?)
▶ help you start thinking phonetically (as in Ma, Lo, Fr, etc.)
▶ give you the first or last letter of the name or word.

In tricky situations when you don't understand, you seek clarification by:

(frown)

▶ asking, 'Is that a place or a person?' – the other person will tell you
▶ frowning and tilting your head slightly
▶ repeating the first letter to show you are trying to work out the word.

These tactics will help you clarify things. For example, if someone is spelling the name of their car and it starts with a 'V', then it can only be one of the following: Volvo, Volkswagen or Vauxhall. It is important that you know the context of the conversation, which will help you understand the fingerspelling.

13.5 Reading fingerspelling: overview

Learning how to relax is critical. If you are relaxed, reading fingerspelling becomes much easier.

One frequently asked question is: '*Do I have to understand it first time?*' The answer is no: no one understands everything first time. It is quite normal to take two or three goes before you understand.

Also, remember there will always be a name of a person or a place that you have never heard of before; there is no shame in not knowing it first time if it's a word with which you are not familiar.

> ● **INSIGHT: LEARNING TIPS**
>
> Practise lip-reading words or names so that you can work out what the fingerspelling is.
>
> Think in words or names rather than letter by letter, and if necessary say the words out aloud.
>
> Use the 'first/last technique' to give you an idea of the word or name.

1 Should you always understand fingerspelling first time?

2 What tactics have you learnt in this section?

3 When you are reading fingerspelling, where should you look?

4 If there is a place beginning with 'Ca', name three possible places.

ANSWERS

1 No – it is normal to take two or three goes.

2 Three: reading phonetically; 'first/last technique'; asking for clarification.

3 Focus on the mouth – with your peripheral vision taking in the hands.

4 Cardiff, Caerphilly, Carlisle.

Note: If you feel you need a break from learning fingerspelling then jump to Chapter 17 ('Starting out with placement'), and then return to Chapter 14 when you are ready to tackle the next phase in learning fingerspelling.

Things to remember

▶ Saying the sounds of the letter groups helps your brain to think phonetically.

▶ Thinking phonetically assists with reading fingerspelling.

▶ The 'first/last technique', i.e. looking for the first and last letters, is a proven and successful way of reading whole words or names.

▶ Our brains make sense of jumbled words.

▶ Knowing if a name is female or male is helpful, as is knowing the context or subject matter (person, place, object).

▶ If you don't understand, seek clarification – avoid asking for a repeat of the fingerspelling only, use a frown and tilt your head slightly.

14 *Fingerspelling signs*

In this chapter you will learn:
▶ *how to fingerspell:*
   ▷ *the days of the week*
   ▷ *members of the family*
   ▷ *cities.*

Some BSL signs are derived from fingerspelling: these are called **fingerspelt signs**. This section will show some of the most widely used ones. These signs need mouthing without voice. Let's start with days of the week.

14.1 Days of the week

Work through the first five days of the week now.

VOCABULARY

Monday	Tuesday	Wednesday

Thursday   Friday

Monday	**'M' tapping twice on the palm**
Tuesday	**'T' tapping twice on edge of hand**
Wednesday	**'W' produced twice in tapping movement**
Thursday	**'T' first then 'H'**
Friday	**'F' with the right hand moving in a clockwise movement**

As you can see, these are all derived from fingerspelling.

Saturday and Sunday are usually signed and not fingerspelt:

Saturday   Sunday

14.2 Members of the family

The following are used for members of the family:

VOCABULARY

mother

Mother: 'M' right hand tapping on left hand (similar to 'Monday'). It is important to mouth 'mother' (without using your voice) to be clear that you are signing 'mother' and not 'Monday'.

father

Father: 'F' tap twice.

REMINDER

It is important to mouth the word at the same time as you are using a fingerspelt sign.

Daughter: 'D' taps twice on left index finger.

daughter

Grandmother: Fingerspell 'G' and 'M'.

grandmother

Grandfather: Fingerspell 'G' and 'F'.

grandfather

 Clip 26

Watch the DVD clip.

14.3 Cities

Some cities are signed: two examples are Leeds and London – these are not fingerspelt. Many other cities or towns tend to be fingerspelt.

VOCABULARY

The following place name signs are based on fingerspelling. Let's start with Newcastle. Fingerspell 'N' and 'C' and mouth 'Newcastle' at the same time.

Newcastle

Cardiff is 'C' and then a double 'F': this uses the **'first/last letter'** technique.

The next three use the 'first and middle letter' rule:

Manchester is 'M' and 'C'.

Middlesbrough is 'M' and 'B'.

Bradford is 'B' and 'F'.

REMINDER

Mouth the name of the town at the same time as fingerspelling.

Other places are part fingerspelt and part signed. The sign for 'mouth' is useful to know for many town names, e.g. Portsmouth, Weymouth and Bournemouth. It is either a simple right index finger making a circle in front of the mouth, or a two-fingered claw shape also making a circle in front of the mouth. Note that the mouth pattern for 'mouth' is 'muth', just as it is when you are using your voice.

Portsmouth uses a combination of fingerspelt 'P' and the sign 'mouth' (mouth 'Portsmouth' at the same time of course):

Portsmouth

Plymouth is the same: fingerspell 'P' and the sign 'mouth'.

Weymouth is similar: 'W' and the sign 'mouth'.

Bournemouth likewise: 'B' and the sign 'mouth'.

Practise all these again, mouthing the names too.

 Clip 27

To see the above examples of fingerspelt signs, look at the DVD clip and practise until you get them right.

● **INSIGHT: LEARNING TIP**

Practise so that you become comfortable using your fingers and hands for fingerspelling as this will help you develop your BSL.

QUIZ

1 Which cities have a sign rather than fingerspelling?

2 How would you sign 'mother'?

3 Is 'Wednesday' one movement or two?

ANSWERS

1 Leeds and London.

2 'M' tapped twice on the palm.

3 Two: 'W' is fingerspelt twice.

WORDS LEARNT IN THIS CHAPTER

Monday	**daughter**	**Bournemouth**
Tuesday	**father**	**Bradford**
Wednesday	**grandfather**	**Cardiff**
Thursday	**grandmother**	**Manchester**
Friday	**mother**	**Middlesbrough**
Saturday		**Newcastle**
Sunday		**Plymouth**
		Portsmouth
		Weymouth

Note: If you feel you need a break from learning fingerspelling then jump to Chapter 17 ('Starting out with placement') and return to the final section (Chapters 15 and 16) on fingerspelling when you feel ready.

Things to remember

▶ To understand fingerspelling it's important to watch the lips.

▶ Most towns or cities have the first initial fingerspelt, e.g. Hastings is fingerspelt 'H'.

▶ Sometimes the first and middle letter are fingerspelt, e.g. Dundee: 'D', 'D'.

▶ Five days of the week have the first letter fingerspelt (Saturday and Sunday are signed).

15 *Using fingerspelling in conversation*

In this chapter you will learn:

▶ *how to use fingerspelling in conversation.*

Often when you first meet someone, you start by sharing names and exchanging personal information, such as where you both live. Fingerspelling is essential to exchange information such as this.

DIALOGUE 15.1

English:	**BSL:**
✳ Hello, what's your name?	✳ hello, name ~~you~~ what?
● My name is Sue.	● ~~me~~ name Sue
✳ Where do you live?	✳ live ~~you~~ where?
● I live in Portsmouth.	● ~~me~~ live Portsmouth

hello

name   ~~you~~   what?

~~me~~   name   Sue

live   ~~you~~   where?

~~me~~   live   Portsmouth

EXERCISE

You have learnt how to fingerspell several place names. Practise the dialogue again using different place names. Here are three more cities for you to use (all follow an 'initial letter twice' rule).

York (use 'Y' letter twice and mouth 'York').

Walsall (use 'W' letter twice and mouth 'Walsall').

Truro (use 'T' letter twice and mouth 'Truro').

Clip 28

Now watch this on the DVD clip.

In the following dialogue you will begin to use the possessive '~~my~~' and '~~your~~', using the clenched fist which points (with palm facing) to the appropriate person. Here '~~my~~' is signed with a fist on the chest as seen in the following illustration, while '~~your~~' points at the other person. Study the illustrations and copy.

~~my~~   ~~your~~

These possessive signs 'mine' and 'yours' are not mouthed words: they indicate what belongs to whom (which is why you will not see them mouthed in the BSL dialogues).

Use your own details in the following dialogue.

DIALOGUE 15.2

English:
* ✴ What is your mother's name?
* ● Her name is ....
* ✴ Where does your mother live?
* ● My mother lives in ....

BSL:
* ✴ ~~your~~ mother name what?
* ● ~~my~~ mother name ....
* ✴ ~~your~~ mother live where?
* ● ~~my~~ mother live ....

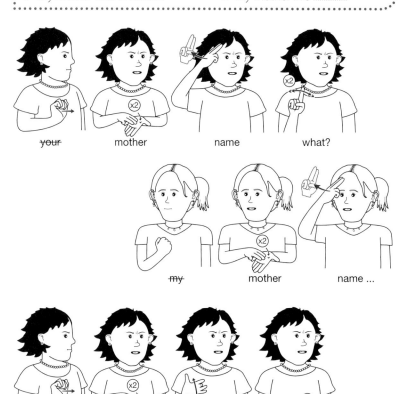

~~your~~   mother   name   what?

~~my~~   mother   name ...

~~your~~   mother   live   where?

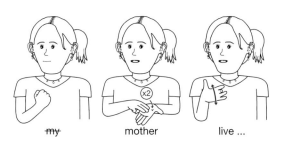

~~my~~   mother   live ...

Complete the dialogue with information relevant to you.

 Clip 29

Watch the DVD clip.

EXERCISE

Now practise the same dialogue using the following words/signs in place of 'mother':

father

daughter

grandfather

grandmother

For example:

'Where does your father live?' (BSL: ~~'your~~ father live where?')

'What is your daughter's name?' (BSL: ~~'your~~ daughter name what?')

We have already introduced all these (fingerspelt) family signs.

Here are some more signs for other members of the family. Practise the same dialogue again:

VOCABULARY

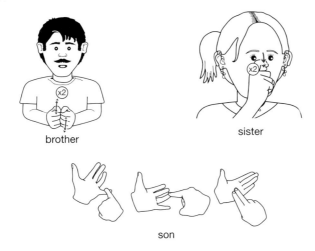

brother

sister

son

 Clip 30

Watch the DVD clip.

WORDS LEARNT IN THIS CHAPTER
brother
my
name
sister
son
your

Things to remember

▶ Possessives in BSL are indicated by a clenched hand (called the 'possessive hand').

▶ The possessive hand is directed to the appropriate person.

▶ You don't usually mouth 'your' or 'my' at the same time as you sign it.

16 *Other fingerspelt words: months*

In this chapter you will learn:

▶ *how to fingerspell the months of the year.*

The months of the year are often spelt in an abbreviated form similar to the way we write them. These are called **fingerspelling patterns**.

VOCABULARY

January is fingerspelt as J A N

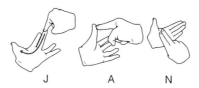

February: F then B

🔘 **Clip 31**

With 'February', you fingerspell 'F' then 'B': but there is a stylized movement which is hard to capture.

Study the DVD in detail.

March: M C H

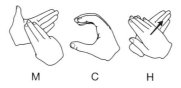

April: fingerspelt as a double 'A' (touch your thumb twice in a circular movement)

May: M A Y

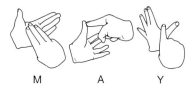

M   A   Y

June: fingerspelt as a short 'J'

J

July: fingerspelt as a long 'J'

J

August: A G

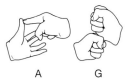

A   G

September: fingerspelt as a double 'S' (tap twice)

S

October: O C T

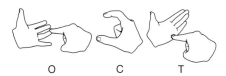

O   C   T

Here is another example of a stylized fingerspelling pattern: the 'O' moves smoothly and without a break into 'C', then morphs into 'T'.

November: N O V

N   O   V

December: D C

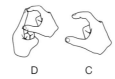

D   C

Practise these several times and then try doing them faster.

 Clip 31

Watch the DVD clip which will show you the flow and rhythm of fingerspelling patterns.

 Clip 32

Look carefully at the sign 'birthday' and watch the dialogue on the DVD.

VOCABULARY

birthday

DIALOGUE 16.1

English:	BSL
✱ When is your birthday?	✱ ~~your~~ birthday when?
● My birthday's in February.	● ~~my~~ birthday Feb
Is your birthday in the same month?	~~you~~ same?
✱ No, it's in December.	✱ ~~me~~ birthday Dec

Vary your sentences using different months so that you have practice with these fingerspelt signs.

REMINDER

Hand-wave or tap on the shoulder to start a conversation.

your   birthday   when?

me   birthday   Feb

you   same?

me   birthday   Dec

'No' is shown by a head shake whilst you point to yourself; then sign 'birthday' and 'December'.

EXERCISE

The signs which we have indicated as 'your', 'me' and 'you' (and similar signs elsewhere) are not translations of these English words: pointing is a way of showing who is the subject of a comment. 'me' means 'I am referring to myself'; this does not have an equivalent in English and is not accurately translated by using the English word 'me'. The crossed-out 'me', 'you', etc. are referent signs.

Now practise the same dialogue but using the following signs
(sign: '~~your~~ father birthday when?' and so on):

father

grandfather

brother

son

daughter

grandmother

sister

 Clip 32

Now watch the DVD clip.

● **INSIGHT: LEARNING TIPS**

Practise the dialogues using the substitute signs so you can ask questions and respond using fingerspelling and signs together.

Think in words or names rather than letter by letter.

QUIZ

1 Which month is fingerspelt with the first initial twice?

2 How are possessive nouns shown in BSL?

3 What do you do with your mouth when fingerspelling?

4 What letters do the digits of your passive hand represent?

ANSWERS

1 April: 'A' 'A'

2 With a clenched fist directed towards the person.

3 You mouth the name or word at the same time.

4 'A', 'E', 'I', 'O', 'U'.

WORDS LEARNT IN THIS CHAPTER

birthday	**January**	**July**
my	**February**	**August**
your	**March**	**September**
	April	**October**
	May	**November**
	June	**December**

Things to remember

▶ Months of the year are fingerspelt.

▶ You need to be able to fingerspell smoothly and fluently.

▶ Possessive signs ('mine', 'yours', etc.) are made towards the appropriate person.

▶ To understand fingerspelling it's important to watch the lips.

17 *Starting out with placement*

In this chapter you will learn:
▶ *what signing space is and how to use it*
▶ *about placement*
▶ *about the eye+hand line.*

17.1 Signing space

We will look at the concept of **signing space** first, and at how Deaf people use this in signing. BSL is a visual language, and the signing space and how it is used are important parts of BSL. Deaf people use their signing space to show where people, places and objects are. This feature of BSL, called **placement**, is difficult to learn but very important. The best advice is to take it slowly and be guided by our exercises.

Before you start, you need to understand fully what signing space means. It is the space in front of you which you use for signing.

FINDING YOUR OWN SIGNING SPACE

Stand relaxed, with both arms bent from the elbows and your hands in front of you.

The whole area in front of you from elbow to elbow, and from your waist to just above your head, is your signing space.

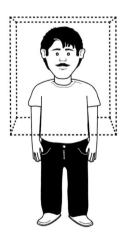

WHY LEARN ABOUT PLACEMENT?

BSL users use their signing space in many ways. Using your signing space correctly not only helps you to understand Deaf people when they use theirs, but also enhances your signing, as good use of signing space adds extra meaning to your signs. You will be using your signing space each time you sign so you will have plenty of practice.

Now let's move on to learn what 'placement' means. Here are some terms to help you:

Placement: Being able to locate objects or people where you visualize them in your signing space.

Signing space: The space you use to sign in.

Eye+hand line: When you are using or placing signs in your signing space, it is important that your eyes follow your hands as you sign. If you are putting something on the shelf, for example, then look at the imaginary object (held in your hand) as you move it and put it on the shelf. The following illustration of a man referring to a cupboard (and therefore looking at it) shows what you need to do:

You now know about signing space and the eye+hand line. These are essential in BSL, so let's practise them with a dialogue.

REMINDER

No voice!

DIALOGUE 17.1

The following dialogue demonstrates the importance of placement in BSL.

English:
* ✱ Good morning, where's your book?
* ● My book's there.
* ✱ Ah is that where your book is? Thank you.
* ● Fine. See you later.

BSL:
* ✱ good morning ~~your~~ book where?
* ● ~~my~~ book there
* ✱ aha! ~~your~~ book ~~there~~ thank you
* ● fine see you later

REMINDER

~~Crossed out~~ words mean you don't need to say them but just point instead. The dialogues are written in BSL.

good   morning

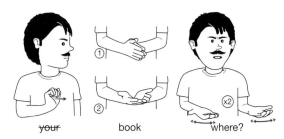

~~your~~   book   where?

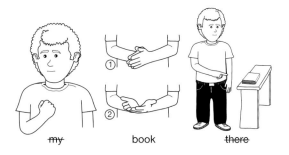

~~my~~   book   ~~there~~

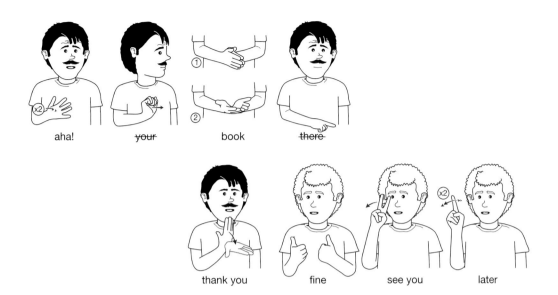

aha!   ~~your~~   book   ~~there~~

thank you   fine   see you   later

Clip 33

Have a look at this on the DVD clip.

● **INSIGHT: CULTURAL TIP**

In BSL, pointing at people or things is an acceptable everyday occurrence. Practise pointing at people and things until you feel comfortable doing this.

● **INSIGHT: LEARNING TIPS**

Practise using the eye+hand line, i.e. looking and pointing at things.

Remember not to use your voice.

Make sure you understand what the 'signing space' is.

REMINDER

BSL is a simultaneous language, as more than one piece of information can be signed at the same time.

WORDS LEARNT IN THIS CHAPTER
book
fine
later
see you

Things to remember

▶ BSL is a visual language using space.

▶ The space you use to sign in is your signing space.

▶ *You* locate objects or people where you visualize them in your signing space using placement.

▶ 'there' is unmouthed.

▶ The eye+hand line means your eyes follow and look at where the signs/objects are in the signing space.

18 Describing a room

In this chapter you will learn:

▶ *how to use spatial language to describe a room.*

Let's start with the kitchen:

VOCABULARY

This is how you sign 'kitchen' and 'cooker'. Have a look below.

kitchen   cooker

In the kitchen on the previous page you can see five cupboards (one with double doors) and three drawers. The signs are very simple: you mime opening the cupboard and mouth 'cupboard', then mime opening the 'drawer' and mouth 'drawer'.

REMINDER

Make the 'opening' an exact movement as if you were opening the individual cupboard or drawer, and don't use your voice.

 Clip 34

Study the DVD clip if you are not sure about these signs.

EXERCISE

Stand at the door of your own kitchen and have a good look around. Remember where everything is. Open the cupboards on the wall and under the sink. Open the drawers, and note what you did and what movements you made.

Now look at the picture of a kitchen again, and imagine you are standing with your back to the cooker. You are looking for some teabags. You open the upper cupboard to your right: the teabags are not there. The next cupboard is to your left so you open the door: you find your teabags!

What did you do?

▸ Did you *move* your hand from right to left as you looked for the teabags?

▸ Did you use both hands when you opened the double door cupboard?

▸ And, did you *look* up as you looked into each cupboard?

It doesn't matter which hand you used. The important thing is you mimed opening each cupboard and you *looked* at where each cupboard was. Remember what was said earlier about the **eye+hand line**. Your eyes must follow your hands: your eye+hand line will show the other person where you are looking.

REMINDER

Remember to look at *where* you are placing things. Because BSL is a visual-spatial language BSL users use the eye+hand line to show exactly where things are.

Let's try another exercise.

EXERCISE

This time you are looking for a spoon: open the top drawer on your left to see if there are any teaspoons. Yes! The spoons are there.

Here is the same picture with more detail:

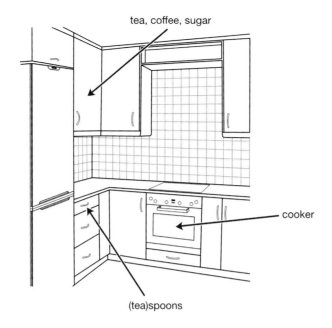

tea, coffee, sugar

cooker

(tea)spoons

VOCABULARY

coffee

tea

milk

sugar

(tea)spoon

Clip 35

Check your new signs on the DVD clip.

Now you know where everything is.

EXERCISE

Imagine you and your friend are facing each other. Your friend is standing with his back to the cooker. You are facing him.

your friend –
with back to cooker

you

You ask your friend: 'Where's the coffee?'

In BSL: 'coffee where?'

coffee   where?

Your friend signs: 'In the cupboard up there.'

In BSL: 'cupboard ~~there~~'

cupboard   ~~there~~

Check the picture of the kitchen. Your friend is pointing to his *right*. You just follow his hand and will know where the cupboard is: yes, you have to look to your *left* to find the coffee. This is why watching where the other person directs their eye+hand line is important. It helps you to work out where the object is.

Go through this exercise again. See how this translates into a conversation with you asking for help to find something:

DIALOGUE 18.1

Remember to wave to attract attention.

English:	BSL:
✱ Do you want some help?	✱ want help?
● Where's the tea?	● tea where?
✱ Up there in the cupboard.	✱ tea cupboard ~~there~~

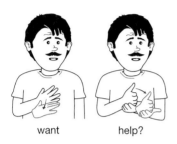

want   help?

tea   where?

tea   cupboard   ~~there~~

Clip 36

Watch the DVD clip.

If you need other things, such as spoons, this is how you ask:

DIALOGUE 18.2

English:
* ✳ Where are the (tea)spoons?
* • In the drawer there.
* ✳ Thank you.
* • No problem.

BSL:
* ✳ (tea)spoon where?
* • (tea)spoon drawer ~~there~~
* ✳ thanks
* • no problem

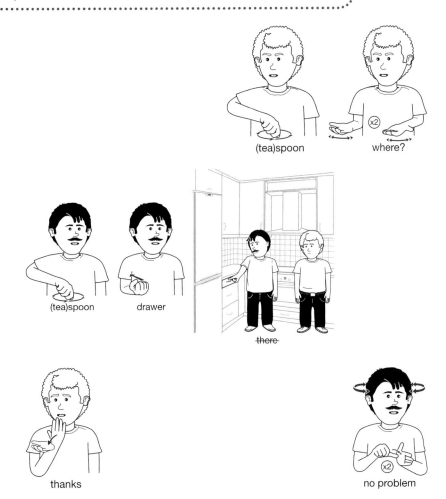

(tea)spoon   where?

(tea)spoon   drawer   ~~there~~

thanks   no problem

EXERCISE

Using the same dialogue, change '(tea)spoons' to other signs: coffee, milk, sugar, tea. Ask the same questions again. Study the illustration so you can give your answers correctly.

🪩 Clip 37

Check your progress with the DVD clip.

Note: This sign for 'spoon' shows that you are asking for one spoon. If you want more than one spoon, add a number: e.g. 'three' spoons. With numbers, make sure your palm is facing you.

three   (tea)spoons

● INSIGHT: LEARNING TIP

Look around your own kitchen and think of where things are, then practise your eye+hand line by pointing and looking at each item in turn. Remember to just look and point: you don't say (or sign) 'there'.

WORDS LEARNT IN THIS CHAPTER

coffee	**milk**
cooker	**no problem**
cupboard	**sugar**
drawer	**tea**
help	**(tea)spoon**
kitchen	**want**

Things to remember

▶ When discussing an item (or person), your hands move to where the thing you are talking about is located.

▶ 'There' is unmouthed.

▶ Use the eye+hand line technique so that your eyes and your hand/s are focused towards the same place.

19 *Introduction to referent handshapes*

In this chapter you will learn:

▶ *how to describe where objects are*
▶ *how to use two referent handshapes: flat hand and 'C' hand.*

19.1 Referent handshapes

Referent handshapes are used in the signing space to *refer* to where different objects or items can be found. You can, for example, demonstrate where an item is without actually being in the room.

Here we introduce two referent handshapes. Practise them until you feel comfortable and also watch the DVD. Remember these are not signs as such, they are handshapes that refer to an object placed in your signing space. Always name the object first. You'll see in a minute how this works.

TWO HANDSHAPES

Flat hand: tends to be linked to flat surfaces, such as wall, table, bed and car.

flat hand

'C' hand: can be used as a reference to how one would handle an item, such as a cup, drink or box.

'C' hand

 Clip 38

Practise these two handshapes now and check them against the DVD clip.

Flat referent handshape

Let's start with the first referent handshape (flat hand), which is often used to represent anything that is flat, for example, bed, plate, table or wall. Check with the illustration above.

Let's see how we can use this referent flat handshape.

In describing a bedroom (when you are not actually in the bedroom) you might want to describe where the bed and other furniture is, so you would say, 'The bed is in the left-hand corner of the bedroom.' In BSL this would be: 'bedroom/bed/there'. This does not seem to have enough detail, but when you sign it, you will be able to convey exactly where the bed is.

VOCABULARY

First you need to sign 'bedroom'. This is a two-part sign so first sign 'bed' and then 'room'.

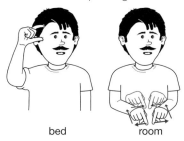

bed   room

To show the size and shape of a bedroom you will need to draw a square (in your signing space) with your closed hands and index fingers extended downwards to represent the bedroom.

Secondly, use the sign for bed.

bed

Thirdly, use the flat referent handshape to place the bed in the room. So use a flat handshape (palm facing down), which represents the bed, and place it in the left-hand corner of the room in the signing space.

If you are somewhere else and you want to explain to someone where the bed is, this is how you would do it:

* Where is the bed?
● The bed is in the left-hand corner.

In BSL you would do it by adding up the signs you've learnt above:

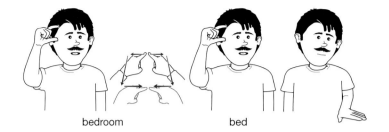

bedroom   bed

Clip 39

Try this a couple of times and have a look at the DVD clip.

'C' referent handshape

The next referent handshape is the 'C', which is for various items that can be held. Many handshapes are created by how we use or hold certain items, for example, 'cup', 'can' (of soup) or 'tin' (of beans).

Look in your kitchen or the local shop and find different types or sizes of cups and cans/tins. Think about how we hold these items. Pick up a tin of beans and put it down somewhere else. Notice the shape your hand makes. We will be using these handshapes in an exercise linked to putting cups, mugs, beakers or tins on shelves.

VOCABULARY

'C' hand   cup   tin

▶ Sign for cup: keep the 'C' handshape whilst pretending you are drinking out of a cup.
▶ Sign for tin: use the 'C' handshape with both hands moving apart to show the size and shape of a tin.

Now using the same 'C' holding handshape, place a cup on a shelf. Imagine you are actually putting a cup on a shelf. Use the holding handshape for cup and move your arm up and put it on an imaginary shelf.

cup

Now put three cups on the shelf. How will you do this? Place three imaginary cups on a shelf: use the same 'C' handshape three times.

ORIENTATION

Showing whether something is upright, lying down, facing outwards (or some other way) is an important skill in BSL. Any referent handshape can also be used to show how an object is placed: upright, on its side, upside down. Remember how you placed the cups on the shelf? Now see if you can show two tins on their sides.

VOCABULARY

You will need the sign for 'plate' for the next exercise. Hold out your passive hand flat and with the index finger of your active hand draw an outline of a plate and mouth the word 'plate' at the same time.

plate

EXERCISE

Can you describe the illustration below of a plate and two tins on their sides?

▶ First sign 'plate', and then use your referent handshape to place the plate on the shelf.
▶ Next sign 'tin' with your two hands, and then using your referent handshape turn your hand to show the two tins lying on their side.

Simply by the correct use of a handshape you can give far more information: 'Here's the plate on the left and here are the two tins on their side, on the right.'

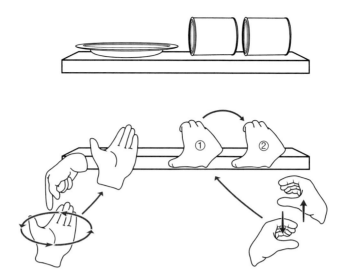

Further work on the 'C' handshape

To make sure you're using the holding 'C' handshape correctly, try this exercise again, this time using a mug.

VOCABULARY

mug

This is how you would show placing a mug upright on the shelf.

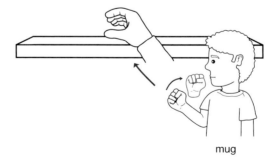

mug

Notice how your sign for mug slowly changes into a 'C' holding handshape moving onto the imaginary shelf.

Clip 40

Try this again and watch the DVD clip.

> **● INSIGHT: LEARNING TIP**
>
> Use your hand+eyeline: look at the mug as you are putting it on the shelf. You cannot look somewhere else whilst putting something on the shelf – it simply wouldn't make visual sense.

EXERCISE: PUTTING A BOX ON A SHELF USING A 'C' HANDSHAPE

We will show you the sign for 'box' and then you will put it on a shelf using skills you have already learnt. You use the same 'C' referent handshape to show how you place a box or a mug on a shelf.

VOCABULARY

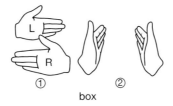

box

▶ First (1) show two sides in front of your body.
▶ Then (2) move your hands to show the other two sides of the box.

Try this complex sign several times to make sure you've got it right by checking with the illustration (and watching the DVD). Pay particular attention to where your palms are facing.

Now you want to describe to a friend where a box is on a shelf so they can go and look for it.
▶ First sign 'box'.
▶ Then use the referent 'C' handshape to place the box on the shelf.

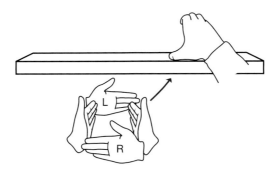

This is tricky, so try it again:

▶ Sign 'box'.

▶ Then, keeping your right hand up, slowly change your handshape into a 'C'.

▶ Move the 'C' handshape onto the imaginary shelf.

🔘 Clip 41

Try this again and watch the DVD clip.

> ● INSIGHT: LEARNING TIP
>
> Use your hand+eyeline, and look at the box as you are putting it on the shelf.

EXERCISE: PUTTING A PLATE ON A SHELF USING THE FLAT REFERENT HANDSHAPE

You've already learnt the sign for 'plate'. This is how to sign 'shelf':

shelf

This is how to sign two shelves:

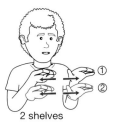

2 shelves

Practise these several times. Now on your own, can you sign three shelves?

Clip 42

Check these signs by watching the DVD clip.

EXERCISE: PUTTING ITEMS ON A SHELF USING REFERENT HANDSHAPES

Here is an open cupboard with items on the shelves:

How you would describe this picture to someone who is not in the room?

▶ First you need to set the scene by drawing the outline of the cupboard using your index fingers to draw a square shape in front of your body.

▶ Then you use the sign for two shelves.

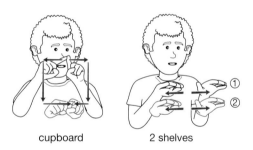

cupboard   2 shelves

You have learnt quite a lot in this chapter – new signs and referent handshapes (flat hand and 'C' hand) so you can describe where things are. Let's now fill up the cupboard!

▶ Sign 'plate' and then use the flat handshape (palm upwards) to put it on the left (make sure it is in the correct place).

▶ Sign 'cup' and use the 'C' referent handshape to place it next to the plate.

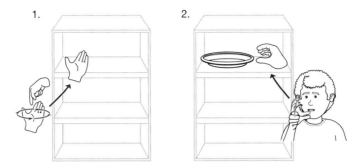

▶ Sign 'tin' and using the 'C' handshape place it below the cup.

▶ Sign 'box' and then use the 'C' handshape to place it next to the tin.

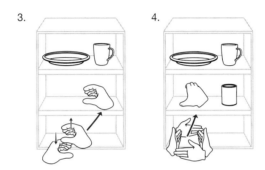

Try this several times as it will take a while to get this right.

DIALOGUE 19.1

Here's a dialogue to show you how this works (remember: tap a person on the shoulder to gain their attention).

English:	BSL:
✷ Where's my plate?	✷ ~~my~~ plate where?
● Your plate is on the shelf.	● shelf plate ~~there~~

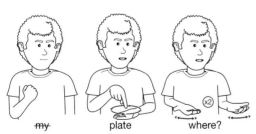

~~my~~   plate   where?

shelf | plate | ~~there~~

REMINDER

Sign 'plate' first and then place it in relation to where the cup is.

English:
* Where's my cup?
• Ah! Your cup is up there on the ~~shelf~~

BSL:
* ~~my~~ cup where?
• ah! you~~r~~ cup ~~there~~

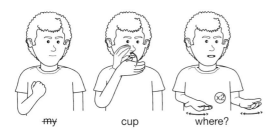

~~my~~ | cup | where?

ah! | ~~your~~ | cup | ~~there~~

EXERCISE

Now sign the following dialogue yourself.

* Where's the tin?
• The tin's there.
* Where's the box?
• The box is there.

💿 **Clip 43**

Watch the clip to make sure you have produced the dialogue correctly.

EXERCISE

The bottom shelf is empty. What else would you put there?

REMINDER

Use the sign for each item and mouth it, e.g. 'tin' or 'box', without using your voice. Then use the referent handshape for all four items ('plate', 'cup', 'tin' and 'box') when you are placing these on the shelves.

Once you have understood the function of these referent handshapes, and also understand them when you see them, it will help you to read what other BSL users are signing about in their signing space.

WORDS LEARNT IN THIS CHAPTER
bed
bedroom
box
cup
cupboard
plate
shelf
tin
two shelves

Things to remember

▸ Referent handshapes are used in the signing space to ***refer*** to where different objects or items can be found.

▸ **The flat hand handshape** is linked to flat surfaces, e.g. wall, table, bed, car.

▸ **The 'C' hand handshape is** used for items that can be grasped, e.g. cup, can, box.

▸ In BSL you always 'name' the object first using the correct sign, before using the referent handshape.

20 *Understanding switching*

In this chapter you will learn:

▶ *how to interpret things from the signer's perspective using switching.*

20.1 Understanding another person

You have already learnt one of the two key principles for understanding signing placement. You simply watch the other person's eye+hand line and follow the direction in which they are pointing, and you point in the same direction. That's not hard: many people automatically point at things, and it is easy to understand what it is they are referring to.

The other key principle is: if you are *not* in the same place looking at the same things from the same point of view, you have to put yourself into the signer's shoes and interpret things from their perspective. This is not so easy, because this means that you need to mentally swap over what you see. What is signed on *their* left, you will see as being on *your* right. This is called **switching**.

Here's a picture to help:

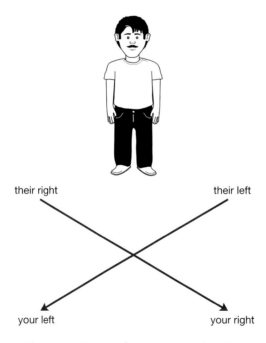

The other person is facing the opposite way from you, so when the signer indicates 'left', their sign is opposite your right, and when they indicate 'right', their sign is opposite your left. Try this out with a friend now: ask them to touch their right arm and you touch your right arm. What happens?

In order to interpret the other person's meaning correctly you need to mentally change places. This **switching** is an essential skill in BSL. Imagine shaking hands with a friend: what happens? Your right hand has to move towards the left as your friend's right hand is diagonally opposite your right hand.

Go back to the two shelves that you looked at in the previous chapter on handshapes. Imagine if these two shelves are in a room that you *cannot* see: perhaps you are in the living room and you have offered to help to bring things from the kitchen to the table, and you ask where the cups and plates are. The person opposite you will be signing as they remember it, which to you will look like this:

But that's not how you will find them when you go into the kitchen looking for the cups and plates – they are the other way round:

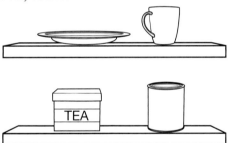

When receiving this kind of description you need to mentally change the objects over (switching) so that you can locate them in the right place.

Now try this out with your own kitchen.

EXERCISE

Here is a game to help you develop this skill – play it with a friend:

▶ You need two packs of cards (one each).
▶ Choose five cards (maybe 1 to 5) from your pack.
▶ Your friend must have identical cards from their pack (if you have the Ace of Diamonds, your friend must have the Ace of Diamonds as well).
▶ Now your friend lays one of their cards down.

- You lay the same card down but in the opposite order (if they lay a card to their left, you lay the same card to your left and so on).
- Then your friend lays another card next to the first card: if they put it to the left of their first card, you put yours to the left as well, and so on.

- Then continue with a third card each etc.
- Try to respond as quickly as possible: sometimes the less time you spend thinking about it, the better!

You will see that although the two rows of cards look different, if you leave the cards on the table and change places with your friend, both sets of cards will be in the same order and location, which is how it should be.

When you've got the concept, you can try the game again using more cards.

QUIZ

Question	Answer
When you point at something – do you have to look at it as well?	Yes
Can you look one way and point in a different direction?	No
Can you use a referent handshape before using the sign?	No
What are the referent handshapes you have learnt so far?	Flat hand and 'C' hand.

Things to remember

▶ Use the eye+hand line to locate objects.

▶ Describe things in their right places and in their right order.

▶ 'Switch' when you are watching a signer describe something you cannot see.

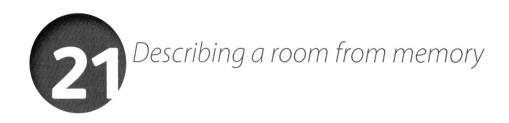

21 Describing a room from memory

In this chapter you will learn:

▶ *how to describe something from memory.*

Now let's develop these skills further. How would you describe a room that neither you nor the person with whom you are speaking are looking at? It could be a room in your home that your friend has never seen.

In BSL you describe it as if you are walking into the room, and, starting at the door, name each item. Start at an obvious point and continue round the room in a logical sequence, remembering to use your eye+hand line. This will help the other person to imagine the layout of your room. If you were to jump around naming and describing items, it would be confusing to the other person as they would not be able to imagine the room in their mind's eye.

EXERCISE

Visualize your bathroom or living room, and work round the room recalling where things are. Remember to place items as you would see them as you look round clockwise (or anti-clockwise).

Now try this. Study this picture of a bedroom:

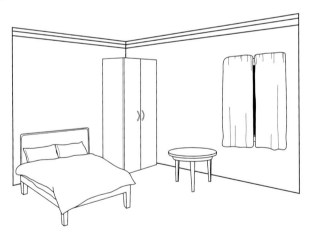

Have a go at describing this room, but let's teach you two new signs first (you already know 'bed', and the sign for 'cupboard' can be used for 'wardrobe' – just mouth 'wardrobe').

VOCABULARY

The sign for 'table': use your flat hands to draw the top and sides of the table.

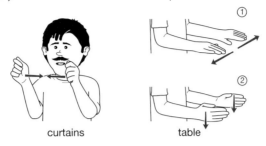

curtains   table

The sign for 'curtains': imagine you are closing the curtains.

Now rehearse all four signs: curtains, table, wardrobe and bed.

Once you've done that, rehearse them again, this time using the appropriate referent sign (and follow the order as in the illustrations):

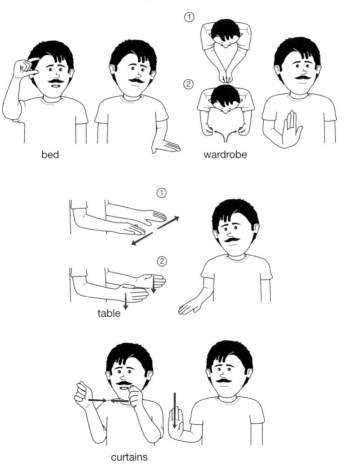

bed   wardrobe

table

curtains

REMINDER

There are **three** steps:

1 Sign the object.

2 Mouth the word at the same time.

3 Then place it in your signing space by using the appropriate referent handshape.

Note: Did you do it in sequence from right to left or from left to right? Either is correct, just remember to do it in a consistent order.

🔊 Clip 44

Watch the DVD clip to see how to describe the bedroom.

You should now be continuously using and developing your signing skills. You should be able to explain to another person where they can find various items in different rooms.

🔊 Clip 45

Watch the DVD clip, which is a dialogue between two people. The first person is describing the bedroom and the second person is trying to understand where things are, and is being corrected when they misunderstand.

EXERCISE

Look at the picture of the bedroom at the start of this chapter again – if the items are signed to you in an anti-clockwise direction (from bed round to curtains) mentally place them in the correct order (from curtains round to bed).

If you are still having difficulty, have another go with the shelves exercise in Chapter 19 ('Introduction to referent handshapes').

EXERCISE

Can you describe another bedroom from memory (either going from left to right, or from right to left), placing the furniture in the right places? If you can do this, then you should be ready to move onto the next chapter.

WORDS LEARNT IN THIS CHAPTER
curtains
table
wardrobe

Things to remember

▶ In order to put yourself in the signer's shoes and see the scene as they see it, you need to master the skill of 'switching'.

22 Understanding someone describing a scene from memory

In this chapter you will learn:

▶ *how to understand another person using BSL*
▶ *about the 'claw' referent handshape.*

The ability to sign in a conversation, explain layouts of rooms etc., requires your use of **productive skills** (you are producing language). If you can understand another person using BSL, the skills involved are called **receptive skills** (you are receiving language).

22.1 The living room scene

Look at this scene from a living room: how would this be described in spoken language? Perhaps: 'On my left is a small table, near the fireplace. The lamp is on the other side of the fireplace with the armchair next to it.'

In BSL a lot of the clues, such as 'on my left', are embedded in the BSL signs, so when the BSL user is standing facing the room, they will describe this scene to you from their left to their right, as: small table, fireplace, lamp, armchair.

REMINDER

You need to use the **switching** skill. When you are watching your friend describing the room, you will see this from your left to your right: chair, lamp, fireplace, small table, so the table is on your right, which is not the correct order (a mirror image of the room layout in fact).

The BSL user will expect you to imagine the scene from their point of view (in spoken language, you are told positions in words: 'in the middle', 'on my right', etc).

EXERCISE

Now switch in your mind so that the items that you see are in the same order and in the same place as the picture (e.g. from your friend's perspective).

22.2 'Claw' referent handshape

Another useful referent handshape to show where things are is the 'claw' handshape. You can use the 'claw' handshape to show where things are in a row, or where objects are scattered about on a table, or furniture placement in a room (you will come across this claw referent handshape again when describing a building or a town later on in this book). It is used below to show the position of the armchair.

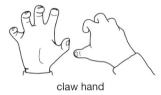

claw hand

VOCABULARY

Here are three new signs you will need: practise 'fireplace', 'lamp' and 'armchair' (along with the sign for 'table' which you have already met). Next to each sign is the referent handshape so you can see how to describe where the furniture is.

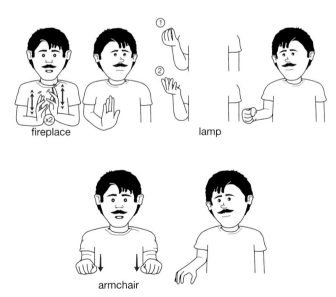

fireplace

lamp

armchair

EXERCISE

Look at the picture of the living room again and remind yourself where the furniture is placed in the room. Now describe the room using the signs and the referent handshapes you have learnt. Remember the order: table, fireplace, lamp, armchair.

EXERCISE: PRACTISE SHOWING UNDERSTANDING WHEN SOMEONE IS DESCRIBING THE ROOM

You previously learnt how to use affirmations (nodding your head) and negations (shaking your head, frowning or tilting your head) to indicate whether you are following what is being signed, and you have used this skill with some of the exercises in earlier chapters.

You should be able to 'place' things correctly in your signing space by copying and describing a room from another person. This is all part of improving your receptive skills.

Now, sign your own rooms from memory: this will help to develop your productive signing skills.

 Clip 46

Watch the living room being described on the DVD clip.

22.3 The street scene

If you are ready, let's look at a street and learn some new signs:

You would sign this street scene (from left to right) as:

restaurant

chemist

newspaper shop

bank

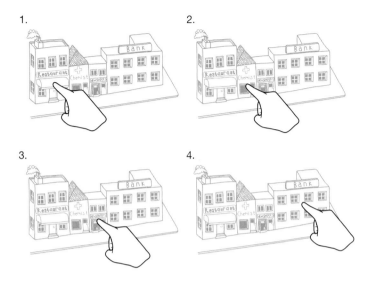

Now study and copy these five signs so that you can begin to describe the street:

VOCABULARY

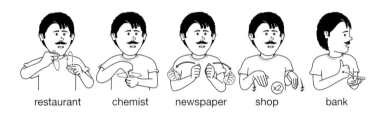

restaurant   chemist   newspaper   shop   bank

When you have described the scene, using your new signs plus claw hand to show where the buildings are, what will the person watching you see – **a** or **b**?

a

bank	newspaper shop	chemist	restaurant

b

restaurant	chemist	newspaper shop	bank

The first one **a** is right: the person watching you will be mentally switching 'left' and 'right' so that they see the shops in the correct order.

 Clip 47

Now watch the street scene being described on the DVD clip.

INSIGHT: LEARNING TIPS
Practise describing places/items in their correct order.

Watch the DVD for examples of placing things in the correct order.

QUIZ

Here are some sentences for you to translate into English:

1 armchair where? (*eyebrows down*)

2 fire ~~there~~? (*eyebrows up*)

3 restaurant where? (*eyebrows down*)

4 newspaper shop ~~there~~ bank ~~there~~

And how would you sign these English sentences in BSL?

5 The curtains are next to the wardrobe.

6 Is the lamp next to the bed?

7 Where are the curtains?

ANSWERS

1 Where's the armchair?

2 Is the fire there?

3 Where is the restaurant?

4 The newspaper shop is there and then there's the bank.

5 wardrobe there, curtains there

6 bed ~~there~~, lamp ~~there~~? (*eyebrows up*)

7 curtains where? (*eyebrows down*)

If you are unsure about the use of eyebrows here, refer to Chapters 6 and 7.

WORDS LEARNT IN THIS CHAPTER
armchair
bank
chemist
fireplace
lamp
newspaper
restaurant
shop

Things to remember

▶ When watching someone 'placing' furniture or buildings, you should use the skill of switching. Remember you need to think diagonally – a bit like when shaking hands.

▶ When describing a room, place things in order: from left to right or right to left; clockwise or anti-clockwise.

▶ Your use of eye+hand lines is essential to help the other person know where things are.

▶ Use referent handshapes correctly.

▶ Use receptive skills to follow a description of a room/scene.

▶ Be confident about pointing at things and be consistent using your eye+hand line to 'place' objects.

▶ Use both hands for placement where appropriate.

▶ Use affirmations/negations to convey whether you have understood.

23 Starting out with directions

In this chapter you will learn:
▶ *how to give and understand directions*
▶ *how to use landmarks*
▶ *how to use the fixed hand.*

23.1 Before you start

In the previous chapters you learnt:
▶ the importance of being able to use and understand the skills of affirmation and negation
▶ how to both use and understand the signing space
▶ how to describe a scene you can see
▶ how to refer to a room or situation you can't see
▶ that handshapes are an essential component of BSL because all sign vocabulary is made up of different kinds of handshapes.

We will be using all these skills again in the next few chapters. In addition, you will learn again the important role spatial awareness plays.

Giving and understanding directions is the next stage of developing your visual awareness. Hearing people give directions by referring to names of streets or places. In BSL directions are given by using visual clues, landmarks and buildings to convey information in a visual way. As you work through the next chapters, continue to pay attention to the structure of the BSL sentences used in the dialogues. There will be an opportunity later to assess your progress in using BSL grammar.

WHY LEARN ABOUT DIRECTIONS?

In BSL, giving and understanding directions are shown visually using your face, facial expression, arms, hands, your signing space and your visual awareness. Chapters 23–26 will take you through the stages of learning these skills.

23.2 Landmarks

In earlier chapters, you learnt how to direct people to find everyday household items, such as coffee or sugar, using pointing, the eye+hand line, and by identifying an obvious feature. Here you will use the same skills but this time the obvious features will be landmarks, such as buildings or a striking part of the landscape.

When giving directions in BSL, identify a landmark that is easily spotted and can be used as a reference point from which to direct people. Try to use a building/shop/statue/crossroads or anything else that is prominent in the immediate environment.

Hearing people use landmarks too in conversation: for example, 'Go down the street and on the left you'll see a pub, turn left there, and there's a church right in front of you, go past that and you'll find the railway station.'

23.3 Fixed hand

When describing the relationship between places, you hold one hand fixed to represent the reference point, then use the other hand to show where the other place is in relation to the fixed hand.

Note: From now on we are assuming:
▶ you know not to use your voice
▶ you will remember how to gain attention and open a conversation.

DIALOGUE 23.1

A friend is asking you for directions to the railway station. 'Good evening' is a new sign for you to learn.

In English: 'Good evening, can you tell me where the railway station is?'

good   evening

station   where?

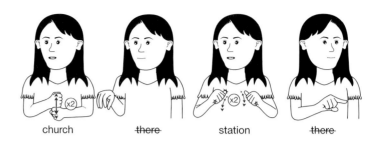

church   ~~there~~   station   ~~there~~

ah!   thank you   ~~fine~~

📀 Clip 48

Watch this dialogue on the DVD.

As you could both see the church, you were able to use this as a landmark to help the person find their way to the railway station. There were three steps to go through:

▶ Identify a landmark that you both can see (the church).
▶ Locate the church.
▶ Point to where the railway station is in relation to the church.

In English, it would go something like this:

'Can you see the church? Go there, and you'll see the railway station on the left.'

This direction is straightforward as both of you are in the same place looking at the same buildings. It is similar to the situation you had before where two people were in the kitchen and one was looking for the coffee (see Chapter 18).

EXERCISE: SPOT THE LANDMARK!

Play this game with a friend.

▶ Pick a street you both know.
▶ Ask the other person to tell you a landmark on the street.
▶ They describe one notable feature of that landmark.
▶ Is the described feature memorable and easily identifiable by anyone?

QUIZ

1 If something is within sight, and you are directing someone, what do you do?

2 Do Deaf people use street names?

3 Do you use the eye+hand line for directions?

ANSWERS

1 Identify the landmark and point to it.

2 Not often – they use landmarks as these are visual.

3 Yes – this is essential.

WORDS LEARNT IN THIS CHAPTER
church
good evening
station

Things to remember

▶ Landmarks are essential to finding your way round.

▶ In BSL directions are given visually rather than verbally.

▶ For directions you need to use the eye+hand line.

▶ Being confident when pointing at people or things means you will be able to give clear directions.

▶ Practise spotting notable landmarks and pointing at them without saying: 'there'.

Directions – describing localities

In this chapter you will learn:

▶ *how to describe a scene.*

24.1 Setting the scene

In this chapter there are some exercises to improve your understanding of signing space and your visual awareness. Work through the exercises (there is a revision section also so you can assess your own learning) and use the DVD to assist you.

In earlier chapters, you learnt about your signing space. The following diagram shows you standing with your signing space in front of you. As you stand and face forwards: A is on your left, B is at an angle on your left, C is at an angle on your right, and D is to your right.

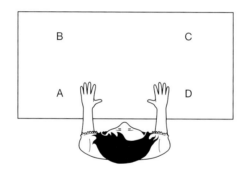

REMINDER

Referent handshapes help you describe where something is. Now use one of the referent handshapes – the claw hand – in the following exercise.

EXERCISE

With your claw hand, show where these four points are in your signing space. Look at the illustrations to help you.

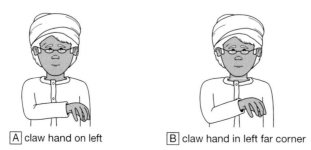

A claw hand on left   B claw hand in left far corner

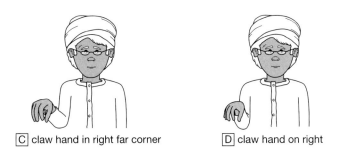

C claw hand in right far corner   D claw hand on right

💿 Clip 49

Watch the DVD clip to make sure you have it exactly right.

Practise the claw referent handshape again without moving your body, but remember to use your eye+hand line correctly. You can use your left hand for the left side and your right hand for the right side as this is more comfortable.

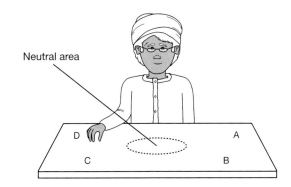

Having set up your signing space, let's see how this links with a map of a village called Deaftown.

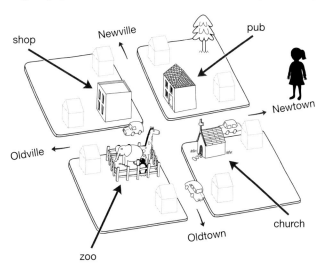

VOCABULARY

Remember you learnt the sign for 'Deaf' in Chapter 2.

The sign for 'new' is the back of your right hand (if you are right handed) brushing upwards against the open palm of your left hand.

The sign for 'old' is your two bent fingers brushing downwards over your nose.

new   old

The sign for 'town' is a claw handshape.

'-ville' is the fingerspelt letter 'V'.

Now practise these signs for the five different places on the map:

Deaftown   Newtown

Newville   Oldtown

Oldville

Clip 50

Watch these new signs on the DVD clip.

As you can see from the map, Deaftown has a few houses and some buildings of local importance, such as the shop and the church. Can you remember the signs for 'shop' and 'church' from previous chapters? If not, here they are again, along with three new signs:

VOCABULARY

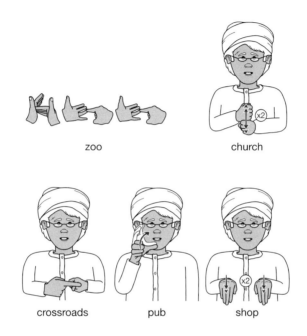

zoo

church

crossroads

pub

shop

Familiarize yourself with the map as this will be used for the next exercise.

If you were facing towards Oldville, standing just before the crossroads, you would place the church to your left in your signing space (A), the zoo would be in your left far corner (B), the shop would be in your right far corner (C) and the pub would be to your right (D).

Clip 51

Watch this on the DVD.

EXERCISE

If you were facing towards Newville: where would the landmarks be? See if you can work it out. Try describing where each of the four landmarks are in your signing space. Can you see how they differ from the earlier exercise?

Did you get it right? If not, have another go. Resist the temptation to skip this exercise as it teaches you an important BSL principle that you will need from here onwards.

Now that you are able to place buildings in your signing space, the next part of this exercise reminds you how to link these buildings by using their names plus a referent claw handshape. Remember the three steps:

1 Use the sign.

2 Mouth the word without voice at the same time.

3 Use the referent claw handshape in the correct place.

zoo

(claw hand placed on left of body)

shop

(claw hand placed at angle to left of body)

pub

(claw hand placed at angle to right of body)

church

(claw hand placed at right of body)

Clip 52

Watch this on the DVD clip.

Repeat this exercise facing a different direction: Oldtown. You will find that once again, while the names are all the same, the locations have changed because you are in a different place and looking in a different direction.

Clip 53

Check how to place these on the DVD clip.

Here is a dialogue using this skill.

DIALOGUE 24.1

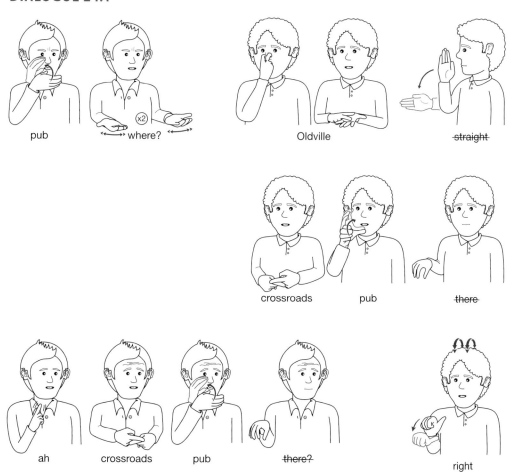

pub   where? (x2)   Oldville   ~~straight~~

crossroads   pub   ~~there~~

ah   crossroads   pub   ~~there?~~   right

Clip 54

Watch the dialogue on the DVD.

24.2 Revision

As we progress through the book, you are learning to combine several things at the same time (remember that BSL is a simultaneous language). We have produced a list for you to study and check against your signing.

Here is a full description of all the aspects of BSL you have been using for this dialogue.

Dialogue	Facial expression	Words mouthed	Words unmouthed	Key BSL feature
pub where?	(eyebrows pulled down)	pub where?		question at the end
Oldville, ~~straight~~ crossroads, pub ~~there~~		Oldville, crossroads pub	straight; there (use claw hand in position D)	use of signing space to place pub in relation to driving onto crossroads
ah crossroads, pub ~~there~~?	(eyebrows up to check if correct)	crossroads, pub	there (use claw hand in position D to confirm)	referent handshape
right	(head nods in affirmation)	right		use of head to show understanding

● INSIGHT: LEARNING TIPS

Practise by using a simple map and setting it out by hand in your signing space.

Think about where local landmarks are and how you would place them in your signing space when facing different directions.

Find a local area you are familiar with; draw locations onto paper, then use your skills to place them in your signing space.

QUIZ

1 Does the placement of a landmark change according to where you are facing?

2 What do you generally put in your neutral area (the space in front of you)?

3 Do you use the eye+hand line for placing the landmarks?

4 What does the sign for church remind you of?

ANSWERS

1 Yes: try turning round in stages and you will find that you are placing the landmark in a different place in your signing space.

2 The most significant area that you can see (in our example the crossroads was used).

3 Yes: this is essential in BSL.

4 Bell-ringing!

WORDS LEARNT IN THIS CHAPTER
crossroads
new
old
pub
straight
town
zoo

Things to remember

▶ Use your signing space to 'place' or 'locate' landmarks.

▶ Placements change according to where you are standing.

▶ Work either clockwise (A → B → C → D) or anti-clockwise (D → C → B → A).

▶ Make use of your eye+hand line.

▶ Name the landmark before using the referent claw handshape.

25 Complex directions: adding more information

In this chapter you will learn:
▶ *how to add information to your description of a scene or directions*
▶ *about the fixed-claw handshape.*

25.1 Landmarks with directions

Now you should be able to place landmarks correctly in your signing space, regardless of the direction you are facing. You will now be able to direct people to where you want them to go using both your hands. One hand will be fixed to anchor the scene, and the other will point the direction.

Here's Deaftown again – but this time it includes extra buildings.

> ● **INSIGHT: LEARNING TIP**
>
> Make an enlarged photocopy of this map so you can refer to it easily as you move through the next two chapters.

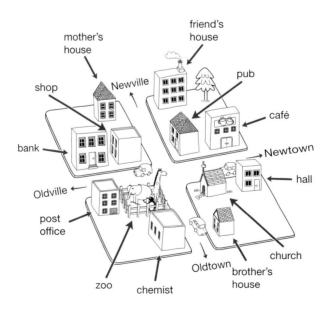

VOCABULARY

Here are some more new signs for this map:

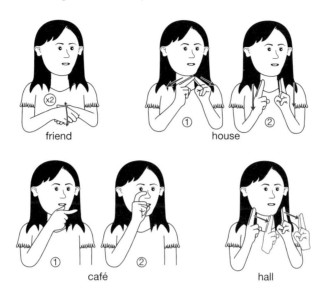

friend

house

café

hall

You already know these, so this is a recap:

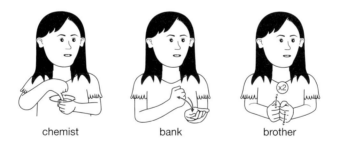

chemist

bank

brother

Clip 55

Check all these signs by watching the DVD.

The following are fingerspelt:

Mother – 'M' ⊗2

Post Office – 'P' then 'O'.

25.2 Fixed-claw handshape

This is a more sophisticated device to show where something unknown is in relation to a known landmark.

Let's suppose you want to show someone who is travelling from Oldtown how to find the village hall. Look at the map again. What you do first is select the easiest landmark – in this case it's the church. Let's look at the first part of the dialogue.

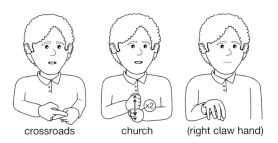

| crossroads | church | (right claw hand) |

Remember: use the claw handshape to show where the church is.

Now you want to show where the church is, so hold your right claw handshape in the same position and keep it there: this becomes the fixed handshape. You then use your left hand over the fixed hand to point to the hall. Try this several times until you get the hang of it.

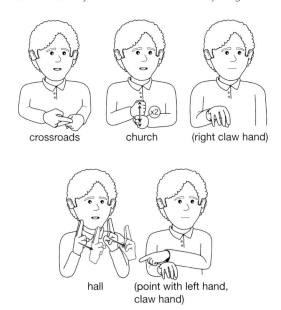

| crossroads | church | (right claw hand) |

| hall | (point with left hand, claw hand) |

Note: You have to release your claw hand to sign 'hall', then revert to the claw hand.

 Clip 56

Now watch this on the DVD.

By using the church as a landmark, it becomes a reference point so the person asking for directions to the village hall will understand where the hall is in relation to the church.

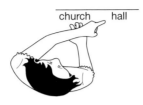

Using a referent handshape in this way to create a relationship between a landmark and another place is called a **fixed hand** because it establishes exactly where you are.

WORDS LEARNT IN THIS CHAPTER
café
friend
hall
house

Things to remember

▶ Use an anchor (fixed hand) sign to give a fixed point for directions.
▶ Give directions from a fixed landmark.

26 Using directions with landmarks

In this chapter you will learn:
▶ *more about giving directions using landmarks, anchoring and placement.*

Study the map in Chapter 25 again.

This time a friend is travelling from Newtown and wants to know where your mother's house is. You would describe it in BSL like this:

crossroads, pub (claw hand on right), ~~my~~ mother's house (point towards right far corner, claw hand)

Use a right-handed claw handshape to **anchor** the pub, and then use your left hand to point out the location of the house relative to this, which as you can see from your signing space is in the right-hand corner away from you.

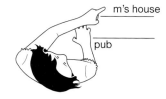

m's house
pub

 Clip 57

Watch this on the DVD as well.

By this stage, you have the basic skills for complex directions:
▶ establishing a landmark in your signing space
▶ anchoring it (using the fixed hand), which sets the scene
▶ placing or pointing with your other hand where you are going next.

Here's a dialogue to cement your learning up to this point. Your friend invites you to come over in the evening. You are aiming for 'friend's house' as seen on the map and you are coming from Oldville.

Friend: 'Are you coming over to my house tonight?'

my   house   tonight

you come?

Your reply: 'Oh yes, I've forgotten where you live?'

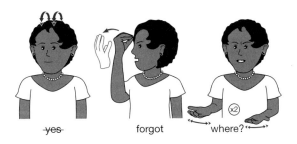

yes   forgot   where?

Friend: 'Go straight towards Newtown, at the crossroads you'll see a shop on your left, my house is opposite, further down.'

straight   Newtown

crossroads   shop   there

my   house   there

Did you remember to use a left-handed claw handshape to anchor the shop, and then use your right hand to point out the location of the house relative to this, which as you can see from your signing space is in the right-hand corner away from the shop?

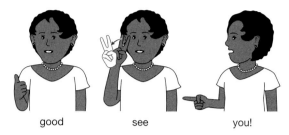

good   see   you!

 Clip 58

Now watch this on the DVD clip.

Things to remember

▶ Represent landmarks using 'anchors' or 'fixed hand', and place other locations in relation to this within your signing space.

▶ Set the scene as *you* see it.

▶ Your eyes and your finger/hand must be aligned towards the same place.

▶ The sign 'my' is mouthed when you need to stress it.

27 Colours

In this chapter you will learn:

▶ *how to sign colours.*

We are now at the end of the book and, after a lot of hard work on your part, we thought we'd treat you to the fun topic of colours. Also, you can use this chapter as a revision exercise for all the BSL grammar you've learnt up to this point.

In this chapter you will learn how to sign colours, which will prove useful in describing different objects (blue cup, red book, yellow plate etc.).

Colours are signed in various ways and they also vary from region to region in the UK. Some of these signs have a visual connection, as you will see in the following illustrations. In this chapter we use the most commonly accepted sign for each colour, but check within your local area for the correct regional sign – it will vary according to where you live. Don't be afraid to learn more than one sign for certain colours.

VOCABULARY

The sign for the word colour is created with a 'C' handshape (using thumb and index finger) in front of the body, moving anticlockwise; and you will need to mouth the word 'colour' at the same time.

colour

Check the illustrations for these colours and practise them. Remember *to mouth the name of the colour when using the sign* (yes, it is a bit like tapping your head and rubbing your stomach at the same time!) Practice makes perfect. It is helpful to check with a Deaf person that you are forming these signs correctly.

Use these colour signs with objects you've learnt in this book, remembering to mouth the name of each colour as you sign.

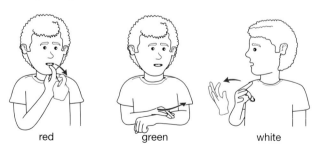

red   green   white

Red: Signed using an index finger, touching the lips first then bending the finger away from the lips and curling it.

Green: Hold your passive arm across your body, with palm facing downwards; and then run your active hand from the wrist towards the elbow finishing on an upward turn.

White: Use the thumb and middle finger of your active hand to make a flicking movement once from your right shoulder.

Clip 59

Check these first three colours on the DVD clip.

REMINDER

Colour signs vary according to where you live!

EXERCISE

Try these out:

1 **English:** The red box is over there.

   BSL: box red *(index finger point)* ~~there~~

2 **English:** Good morning, see you by the white shop.

   BSL: good morning white shop see ~~you~~ *(index finger point)* ~~there~~

3 **English:** My friend's name is Sue Green.

   BSL: friend name, *(fingerspell)* Sue, Green

Clip 60

Check the BSL on the DVD clip.

VOCABULARY

Here are three more colour signs.

Clip 61

Remember to study the DVD clip.

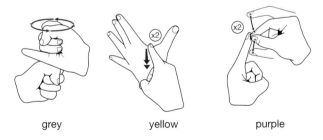

grey   yellow   purple

Grey: This sign uses two clenched hands (one with outstretched little finger), one on top of the other, making two anti-clockwise movements.

Yellow: Use the fingerspelt letter for 'Y'. Touch the base of the 'Y' twice with your right index finger and mouth the word 'yellow'.

Purple: Use the fingerspelt letter 'P' and flick the index finger twice.

EXERCISE

Put these English sentences into BSL:
- ▶ The sugar is in the yellow cupboard.
- ▶ Good afternoon, see you by the purple shop.
- ▶ The grey TV in the shop is the same as mine.

📀 Clip 62

Check the signs for these three colours and for the three sentences on the DVD clip.

VOCABULARY

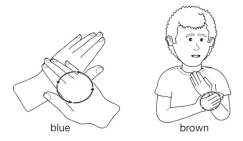

blue   brown

Blue: Rub the fingertips of your active hand (in a horizontal position) on the back of your passive hand.

Brown: Hold your left forearm loosely across your chest. Make a circular stroking motion on your left forearm with your right (flat) hand.

EXERCISE

How would you sign these?
- ▶ The tea is in the blue teapot.
- ▶ My married sister's bike is brown.

📀 Clip 63

Now check the signs for blue and brown, and these sentences in BSL, on the DVD clip.

VOCABULARY

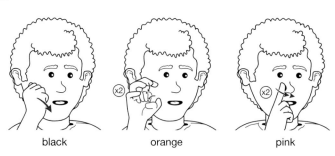

black   orange   pink

Black: This sign is made with a clenched fist touching your cheek, making one straight movement forward.

Orange: Use a 'claw' handshape next to your mouth (palm facing outwards) and make a gentle movement, like squeezing an orange.

Pink: Make this sign with your index finger – stroke the side of the tip of your nose forwards twice.

Gold: Start with the fingerspelt letter 'G', move your hands slightly apart, and then both hands spring open.

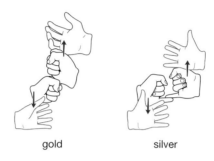

gold   silver

Silver: This one is a bit trickier but try it out! You need to have both hands ready to fingerspell the letter 'S', and then, as you bring them together to make the letter 'S', both hands spring open.

Clip 64

Check the signs for these last five colours on the DVD clip.

Use these dialogues to revise what you have learnt in this book:

DIALOGUES 27.1

	English:	BSL:
Q:	Where is my blue book?	~~my~~ book blue where?
A:	Your blue book is on the shelf in the kitchen.	~~your~~ book blue kitchen shelf (*point*) ~~there~~
Q:	Where's the yellow mug?	mug yellow where?
A:	The yellow mug is on the table.	table, (*point*) ~~there~~ (*if you can see the mug there's no need to add 'yellow mug'*)
Q:	What colour is your kitchen?	~~your~~ kitchen colour what?
A:	My kitchen is orange.	~~my~~ kitchen orange (*head nod*)
Q:	Please can I have four green plates?	please give four plates green
Q:	Is the colour in your bedroom pink?	~~your~~ bedroom colour pink?
A:	No, it is white.	~~no~~ (*headshake*) white (*headnod*)

● **Clip 65**

Check the BSL for the dialogues on the DVD clip.

WORDS LEARNT IN THIS CHAPTER

black	**orange**
blue	**pink**
brown	**purple**
colour	**red**
gold	**silver**
green	**white**
grey	**yellow**

Things to remember

▶ Different signs for some colours are used in different regions.

▶ Some of the colour signs have a visual connection, but some do not.

▶ Mouth the name of the colour at the same time as signing it.

What next?

In this chapter you will learn:

▶ *where to go next to further your learning.*

Having worked through this book, you will want to think about your next steps. As this is an introduction to British Sign Language, you have covered the following elements:

▶ signing space
▶ placement
▶ referent handshapes
▶ facial expressions
▶ mouth patterns
▶ signs that change according to speed, direction and movement.

These will stand you in good stead in developing a wider vocabulary as well as greater fluency.

You can surf the internet (including YouTube) for video clips of BSL to watch. However, do bear in mind the following:

▶ Some signs will be regional.
▶ Some clips will be of a much higher standard than you are accustomed to and should be used for information gathering rather than learning signs.
▶ Some clips will be poor and may not have any of the elements that you have learnt.
▶ Some clips will have been prepared by hearing people and may not look quite right.

● INSIGHT: LEARNING TIPS

Some local councils' information websites provide transcripts along with their signed versions.

You may feel confident enough to want to try to use your new-found skills to see if you can meet some Deaf people. Here are some suggestions:

▶ Go to an event with a friend for company – there's nothing worse than standing around in a crowd and not understanding anyone.
▶ Try to go to something that you have an interest in, e.g. sport, religion or a hobby – you will have something to discuss.
▶ See if you can volunteer at a local school that uses signs, or for a project that requires volunteers who have some signing skills already.

There are several societies or organizations that work with or for Deaf people. These are often good places to meet like-minded people, and you may be lucky enough to find opportunities to practise what you have learnt. Many are easily found in the Yellow Pages or on the internet.

There are some national organizations that work with Deaf people who use BSL. For information and possible routes to meeting Deaf people, as well as a number of video clips depicting Deaf people using BSL, look up the British Deaf Association: www.bda.org.uk. They also organize the annual 'Learn to Sign' week, and you may be able to join in an activity. For Deaf children, there is the National Deaf Children's Society, who welcome volunteers (www.ndcs.org.uk).

If you have worked through this book, you will have the essential elements for successful development of your BSL. Different qualifications in BSL are offered by both the British Deaf Association (BDA) and Signature. If you want to develop your skills to obtain a qualification in BSL, you could join a local adult day or evening class in BSL (or other courses organized locally):

▶ Contact the British Deaf Association (www.bda.org.uk) for a list of its accredited BSL courses around the UK.
▶ The Signature website (www.signature.org.uk) has its own list of BSL courses in the UK.

Both BDA and Signature websites will also provide you with details of their BSL qualifications.

If you are a BSL tutor, you may have found this book helpful; if so, use it for reference and do recommend it to your students!

Index

Signs (words) are in normal font.

Topics are in *italics*

Notes

Notes